Mastering Persuasion

NLP Techniques for Legal Influence and Connection in the Courtroom

By

Shannon Meade

Disclaimer:
The information contained in this book is for educational and informational purposes only. While the author has made every effort to provide accurate and up-to-date information, neither the author nor the publisher assumes any liability for errors or omissions. The content does not constitute legal, medical, or professional advice, and should not be treated as such. Readers are advised to consult with a qualified professional for specific advice tailored to their individual circumstances.

This publication is provided "as is" without any representations or warranties, express or implied. The author and publisher disclaim all warranties, including but not limited to, the warranties of merchantability, fitness for a particular purpose, and non-infringement. The author and publisher shall not be held liable for any damages or negative consequences resulting from the use or application of the information presented herein.

Title & Author: *Mastering Persuasion: NLP Techniques for Legal Influence and Connection in the Courtroom*/ Shannon Meade, JD, LL.M
ISBN: 979-8-89619-252-7
Published by: Shannon Meade
Printed in the United States of America

For permissions, please contact:

Shannon Meade
PO Box 158
Machiasport, Maine

To those who seek justice with integrity and wield influence with humility. May this work serve as a guide not only to sharpen your skills but also to deepen your compassion and commitment to the ideals that underpin our legal system.

Preface

Congratulations on finding this book. By holding it in your hands, you've taken the first step toward an exceptional journey in mastering influence, communication, and connection in the courtroom—skills that set apart the truly distinguished legal professionals from the merely competent. The techniques you are about to learn are powerful. They represent years of insight and refinement in the study of Neuro-Linguistic Programming (NLP) as applied to legal practice, and they hold the potential to profoundly enhance your effectiveness in trial lawyering.

But let me advise you: tell no one about this book. The wisdom within is not for boasting or display, and these skills are best learned quietly, practiced in silence, and wielded with discretion. Your success will not be in the overt demonstration of influence but in the subtle, nearly invisible ways you can guide a jury, connect with a witness, or persuade a judge without ever seeming to. True mastery lies in the subtlety of your craft and your ability to shape interactions without drawing attention to the tools you're using.

With these techniques, you have the opportunity to become a practitioner of immense skill. Yet, with power comes responsibility—and danger. The ethical use of this knowledge is paramount. These techniques can easily be misused, becoming instruments of manipulation rather than tools for justice. I urge you, therefore, to proceed with caution. The temptation to misuse these skills may arise, but the integrity of your practice and the respect you owe to the bar, the tribunal, your clients, and witnesses must remain at the forefront. Power, when abused, will not go unnoticed, and the consequences can erode the very foundations of trust that you seek to build.

Remember your commitment to justice, to compassion, and to fairness. Each case you handle, every client you represent, and every moment you spend in court is an opportunity to serve these ideals. You have an ethical obligation to conduct yourself with the highest integrity—to be not just a fierce advocate, but a principled one. Your clients, the court, and ultimately, society, depend on your ability to balance skill with ethics, influence with honesty, and power with compassion.

In the end, the techniques shared in this book are merely tools. It is up to you to wield them wisely, pursuing justice with a heart guided by empathy and a mind focused on integrity. As you embark on this path, know that true influence comes not from control but from understanding, not from manipulation but from mastery. Use what you learn here to become a better lawyer and, above all, a better servant of justice.

Shannon Meade

5. MASTERING THE SUBTLETIES: ADVANCED NON-VERBAL TECHNIQUES FOR INSIGHT AND INFLUENCE 113

9. NLP TECHNIQUES FOR CALENDAR NEGOTIATIONS: BUILDING INFLUENCE BEYOND THE COURTROOM

1. Mastering the Foundations of NLP: A Comprehensive Guide for Legal Professionals

Neuro-Linguistic Programming (NLP) is a psychological approach that explores the relationship between language, behavior, and the mind to enhance communication, influence, and personal development. NLP's foundations lie in the work of Richard Bandler and John Grinder, who developed the system in the 1970s by studying the techniques of successful therapists and communicators. The framework is built upon several fundamental principles, including understanding how people perceive and process information through various representational systems such as visual, auditory, and kinesthetic modes. At its core, NLP aims to improve rapport-building, sensory acuity, and calibration—key skills that allow individuals to read and adapt to others effectively. Techniques like anchoring and working with submodalities also play a crucial role in creating and managing emotional states. In the legal field, NLP offers powerful applications, helping lawyers adapt their communication strategies to connect with jurors, witnesses, and judges. Understanding these foundational concepts equips legal professionals with tools to navigate complex interactions and influence courtroom outcomes more effectively.

Foundations of NLP: Building Blocks of Influence and Mastery

Neuro-Linguistic Programming (NLP) has emerged as a transformative tool, especially for professionals in fields where communication and influence are paramount. This section delves into its origins, development, and fundamental principles, laying the groundwork for understanding how NLP can be leveraged in legal practice.

History and Development of NLP: From Therapy Rooms to Courtrooms

The Beginnings: How Two Minds Shaped a New Discipline

In the 1970s, Richard Bandler, a mathematician and computer scientist, teamed up with John Grinder, a linguist, to explore the mechanics behind effective communication and therapeutic change. The duo was fascinated by how certain therapists achieved remarkable results while others struggled. They set out to decode the patterns and strategies these experts used, systematically observing and modeling their behaviors.

Bandler and Grinder's initial work involved studying figures like Milton H. Erickson, Virginia Satir, and Fritz Perls. Erickson's use of hypnotic language, Satir's family therapy techniques, and Perls' Gestalt methods became the cornerstone of NLP's early development. The duo aimed to capture the essence of these practices, distill them into replicable patterns, and build a comprehensive framework that could be taught to others.

The Core Principles: Modeling Excellence

Bandler and Grinder discovered that by analyzing and replicating the behaviors, language patterns, and thinking processes of successful people, they could teach others to achieve similar results. This concept, known as "modeling," became the backbone of NLP. Modeling involves breaking down complex behaviors into their components— understanding what a person sees, hears, and feels when they perform a particular skill. The idea is that if you can "model" the internal and external strategies of a successful

2

individual, you can replicate and transfer that success to others.

For trial lawyers, this is particularly powerful. By studying the behaviors, gestures, and language patterns of accomplished attorneys, you can adopt these same strategies in your courtroom performance, negotiations, or witness examination.

The Growth and Expansion: From Therapy to Influence and Beyond

What began as a therapeutic tool quickly expanded into various domains, including business, sports, education, and law. NLP evolved beyond therapy to become a versatile methodology for enhancing performance and communication. Bandler and Grinder realized that NLP's principles could be applied wherever people interact, making it relevant for fields like trial lawyering, where persuasion, communication, and influence are critical.

The Structure of NLP: Mapping the Mind for Mastery

The Communication Model: How We Perceive the World

At the heart of NLP is its communication model, which explains how individuals perceive and interpret the world around them. This model proposes that our experiences are filtered through sensory input systems—visual, auditory, kinesthetic, olfactory, and gustatory—before being processed by our minds. However, not all this information reaches our conscious awareness. The mind filters it based on beliefs, values, past experiences, and language. This process creates our internal representation of reality.

Imagine a scenario in a trial: you present a compelling piece of evidence, but each juror perceives it differently based on their unique filters. One juror may focus on the visual aspects of the evidence, while another may be more attuned to the auditory details of witness testimonies. Understanding this variability allows you to adjust your presentation style to resonate with all sensory modalities, ensuring that your message reaches each juror effectively.

Representational Systems: The Language of the Mind

NLP categorizes how people process information into primary representational systems: visual, auditory, and kinesthetic. Each person has a dominant system they rely on when thinking or communicating. For example:

- **Visual Thinkers**: These individuals often use phrases like "I see what you mean" or "Let's look at the big picture." They respond well to visual cues such as diagrams, gestures, or imagery.
- **Auditory Thinkers**: They use phrases like "I hear you" or "That rings a bell." They are influenced by tone of voice, rhythm, and the clarity of spoken information.
- **Kinesthetic Thinkers**: They might say, "This feels right" or "I can't quite grasp it." They rely on physical sensations, emotions, and tactile experiences.

For trial lawyers, identifying a juror's or witness's primary representational system can be invaluable. For instance, during jury selection (voir dire), paying attention to the language jurors use provides clues about their dominant systems. If you identify a predominantly visual juror, you can enhance your impact by emphasizing visual evidence and using descriptive language that paints a vivid picture.

Key Concepts of NLP: Unlocking the Mechanics of Influence

Rapport: The Glue of Connection

Building rapport is the foundation of effective communication and influence in NLP. It's the ability to create a sense of trust, connection, and understanding with others, even when no words are exchanged. Bandler and Grinder observed that people who are in rapport tend to mirror each other's body language, tone of voice, and even breathing patterns.

Step-by-Step Guide: Establishing Rapport in Legal Settings

1. **Observe Non-Verbal Cues**: Notice the posture, gestures, and expressions of the person you're interacting with. In a courtroom, this could be a judge, a witness, or a juror.
2. **Match and Mirror**: Subtly mirror their body language and gestures. If a judge leans back, you might mirror this posture briefly before transitioning into a more open stance as you present your case.
3. **Pace and Lead**: Once rapport is established, begin to lead the interaction. For instance, if you mirror a DA's speech pace during negotiations, gradually shift the pace to emphasize your point, leading them into agreement.

By mastering rapport, you can subtly influence others without appearing manipulative, ensuring that you are perceived as genuine and trustworthy.

Sensory Acuity and Calibration: Reading the Subtleties

Sensory acuity is the skill of detecting minute changes in others' physiology—such as changes in breathing, skin color, or eye movement—that indicate shifts in their emotional or mental states. Calibration involves adapting your behavior based on these observations to maintain rapport or influence.

Practical Application: Using Sensory Acuity in Witness Examination

During cross-examination, a skilled lawyer uses sensory acuity to pick up on micro-expressions or physiological changes in a witness. For example:

- If a witness shifts in their seat or avoids eye contact when asked a specific question, this may indicate discomfort or evasion.
- Calibration involves adjusting your questioning style or posture to either confront this behavior directly or ease the witness back into a state where they're more likely to answer truthfully.

Mastering sensory acuity and calibration allows lawyers to respond in real-time, adapting strategies based on the subtle cues provided by witnesses, jurors, or even opposing counsel.

Anchoring: Creating Emotional States on Demand

Anchoring is the process of associating a physical gesture or verbal cue with a specific emotional state. Once established, this anchor can be triggered to recreate that emotional state at will.

Script for Establishing an Anchor for Confidence During Trial

1. **Recall a Moment of Confidence**: Close your eyes and recall a moment when you felt incredibly confident.

Make this image as vivid as possible—focus on what you saw, heard, and felt.

2. **Choose a Physical Gesture**: While in this state, perform a subtle gesture (e.g., pressing your thumb and forefinger together).

3. **Repeat and Reinforce**: Repeat this process multiple times until the gesture consistently triggers the feeling of confidence.

4. **Use the Anchor**: In moments of high stress during a trial (e.g., delivering an argument or responding to an objection), use the gesture to instantly access this confident state.

Applications of NLP in Law: Turning Theory into Practice

Adapting NLP Techniques for the Courtroom

The courtroom is a dynamic environment where influence, perception, and communication are essential. NLP offers a toolkit that can be adapted to enhance trial performance, negotiations, and interactions with jurors. By understanding how people perceive information through their dominant representational systems, lawyers can tailor their arguments to resonate with each individual's processing style.

For example, when delivering a closing argument, a lawyer might:

- Use **visual language** and gestures for jurors with a visual processing style ("Picture the scene as it happened...").
- Incorporate **auditory elements** such as varying tone and pace for auditory-oriented jurors ("Listen carefully to the facts...").
- Engage **kinesthetic jurors** by emphasizing feelings and physical actions ("Feel the weight of responsibility as you consider...").

By employing these strategies, you maximize your influence and ensure your message is received clearly by all jurors, enhancing your chances of a favorable verdict.

Calendar Negotiations and Motion Hearings: The Influence Advantage

Outside the courtroom, NLP's principles are equally powerful. Whether negotiating with DAs or arguing motions before a judge, understanding and leveraging rapport, pacing, and language patterns allows for more effective and persuasive communication.

For instance, during a calendar negotiation:

- **Pace** the DA's concerns by acknowledging their busy schedule and aligning your language with their priorities.
- **Lead** the conversation towards mutually beneficial solutions by subtly reframing the negotiation as a way to streamline both of your workloads.

By integrating these principles, NLP becomes an invaluable tool, enhancing your effectiveness across all areas of legal practice.

This comprehensive understanding of the foundations of NLP provides the groundwork for mastering the advanced techniques that will be explored in subsequent sections, ensuring that you become not only a proficient communicator but an expert in using NLP for maximum influence and success in the legal profession.

The NLP Communication Model: Decoding How We Experience the World

The NLP Communication Model is the foundation for understanding how humans perceive and process information. This model explains how external stimuli are transformed into our internal reality, influencing our behavior, decisions, and communication. In legal contexts, this model is crucial because it reveals how jurors, witnesses, judges, and opposing counsel interpret information, providing a strategic advantage in crafting messages that resonate and persuade.

How We Experience Reality: The Filters That Shape Perception

The Journey of Information: From Sensory Input to Internal Representation

Imagine standing in a courtroom, observing a witness recount a crucial event. The words they choose, the tone of their voice, and their gestures all convey information. However, the way each juror perceives this testimony differs. This variation occurs because, according to NLP, every individual processes information through a unique set of filters that shape their internal experience of reality.

When we encounter any event, our senses—visual (sight), auditory (hearing), kinesthetic (touch/feeling), olfactory (smell), and gustatory (taste)—collect information. This sensory input is vast and complex, but our minds cannot process everything at once. To make sense of the world, our brain filters this information using our beliefs, values, past experiences, and language patterns. These filters act as a lens through which we perceive reality, transforming raw data into a personalized internal representation.

For instance, two jurors may hear the same witness testimony, but one focuses on the visual cues (the witness's facial expressions), while the other is more attuned to the auditory elements (the witness's tone of voice). This discrepancy explains why jurors may interpret evidence differently, making it crucial for attorneys to adapt their presentation style to engage all representational systems.

The Filters in Action: Beliefs, Values, and Language

In the legal field, understanding these filters becomes a strategic advantage. A juror's belief system, shaped by their cultural background or life experiences, may influence how they perceive a defendant's behavior. A lawyer who understands this can tailor their argument to align with the juror's values or reframe information to bypass biases.

For example, during a motion hearing, if a judge is known to value efficiency and justice, an attorney could frame their argument to emphasize how granting the motion would serve these principles. By aligning with the judge's filters, the attorney increases the likelihood of a favorable outcome.

Representational Systems: The Different Languages of the Mind

Visual, Auditory, and Kinesthetic Systems: Understanding How People Think

One of the most powerful insights from the NLP Communication Model is the concept of representational systems—how people use their senses to experience the world and communicate. NLP identifies three primary systems: visual, auditory, and kinesthetic. Each individual tends to favor one system, influencing how they think, speak, and respond.

Visual Thinkers: The Power of Imagery

Visual individuals process information primarily through sight and imagery. They often use phrases like "I see what you mean" or "Let's look at the evidence." They are typically fast-paced thinkers who visualize concepts and scenarios in their minds. In the courtroom, visual jurors respond well to exhibits, diagrams, and visual storytelling techniques that help them "see" the argument.

Practical Application: Engaging Visual Thinkers in Trial

1. **Use Visual Aids**: When presenting evidence, employ charts, graphs, or visual recreations of events. Visual thinkers will be more engaged when they can connect concepts with images.
2. **Descriptive Language**: In closing arguments, use imagery-rich language: "Imagine the scene as it unfolded, the defendant standing with clear intent..." This paints a mental picture that visual jurors can latch onto.
3. **Body Language**: Maintain eye contact and use deliberate gestures when addressing the jury. Visual people pick up on and respond to these cues.

Auditory Thinkers: The World Through Words

Auditory individuals process information primarily through sounds and verbal language. They tend to use phrases like "That sounds right" or "I hear you." These individuals are sensitive to tone, rhythm, and inflection, making them particularly responsive to verbal arguments and the way information is delivered.

Script for Connecting with Auditory Jurors During Closing Argument

- **Opening Line**: "Listen closely to the evidence presented and pay attention to the words of each witness."
- **Tone Variation**: Modulate your voice to emphasize critical points, such as raising your pitch slightly when making a crucial argument or lowering it to create a sense of seriousness.
- **Repetition**: Reinforce key points with repetition to anchor the information: "Remember what you heard—the facts are clear."

By consciously varying your tone and emphasizing key auditory elements, you ensure that auditory jurors receive and internalize your message effectively.

Kinesthetic Thinkers: Feeling the Facts

Kinesthetic individuals connect with the world through feelings, touch, and physical experiences. They often use language like "This doesn't feel right" or "I need to get a grip on the details." These thinkers are slower-paced, focusing on physical and emotional cues rather than visual or auditory information. In a legal context, engaging kinesthetic jurors involves creating an emotional or tactile connection to the case.

Strategies for Engaging Kinesthetic Jurors

1. **Emotionally Charged Narratives**: Tell stories that evoke feelings, such as describing the emotional impact on a victim or the physical sensations involved in an event. "Imagine the fear they felt, the weight of that moment..."
2. **Physical Anchors**: Use gestures that evoke physical experiences—such as touching your chest when speaking of sincerity or leaning forward when describing intensity.
3. **Slow and Deliberate Speech**: Kinesthetic individuals respond to slower pacing. By slowing down your delivery, you allow them to connect with the emotional weight of your words.

Integrating Representational Systems in Legal Practice: A Holistic Approach

In practice, it's essential to engage all three representational systems when interacting with jurors, witnesses, or judges. Most people use a combination of systems, and ensuring that your communication touches on each one maximizes your impact.

Practical Guide: Engaging All Representational Systems During Opening Statements

1. **Visual Engagement**: Start with a vivid description of the scene: "Picture the street at dusk, the headlights cutting through the fog."
2. **Auditory Elements**: Integrate sounds into your narrative: "You can hear the screech of the tires, the shouts of witnesses."
3. **Kinesthetic Connection**: Finish with a physical or emotional touch: "Feel the tension in the air, the weight of what's at stake."

By weaving these elements together, you create a multi-sensory experience that engages the entire jury, increasing the likelihood that your message resonates deeply.

Advanced Techniques: Identifying and Adapting to Representational Systems

Reading the Clues: How to Identify Someone's Representational System

In any interaction—whether it's with a juror, witness, or judge—identifying their primary representational system allows you to tailor your approach for maximum effectiveness. People provide clues through their language, eye movements, and body language.

- **Language Cues**: Listen for specific phrases. Visual people often say "see" or "picture," auditory individuals use "hear" or "say," and kinesthetic people mention "feel" or "grasp."

- **Eye Accessing Cues**: In NLP, the direction of a person's eye movements can indicate which representational system they are using:
  - **Upward Movement**: Visual processing.
  - **Sideways Movement**: Auditory processing.
  - **Downward Movement**: Kinesthetic or internal dialogue.
- **Body Language**: Visual individuals may have a more upright posture, auditory people might tilt their heads, and kinesthetic individuals often lean forward, emphasizing a sense of physical involvement.

Scripts for Identifying and Adapting to Representational Systems

1. **Identifying**:
   - Ask an open-ended question like: "How do you prefer to process information—by seeing things, hearing about them, or getting a sense of how they feel?"
   - Observe their eye movements and posture while they respond, noting any dominant tendencies.
2. **Adapting**:
   - For a visual person: "Let's take a look at the evidence and visualize how it all fits together."
   - For an auditory person: "Listen closely to the testimony as I walk you through the details."
   - For a kinesthetic person: "Imagine how the defendant must have felt in that moment."

The Power of the NLP Communication Model in Legal Practice

The NLP Communication Model is a blueprint for understanding and influencing how people perceive and respond to information. By mastering the art of identifying and adapting to different representational systems, legal professionals can tailor their communication strategies to resonate deeply with jurors, witnesses, judges, and opposing counsel.

Whether delivering a powerful closing argument, negotiating a calendar date with a DA, or cross-examining a witness, the ability to align your message with an individual's internal processing system is a game-changing skill. With these tools, you can create compelling, multi-sensory narratives that captivate your audience and maximize your effectiveness in every legal setting.

Key Concepts of NLP: The Tools for Mastering Communication and Influence

The core of Neuro-Linguistic Programming (NLP) lies in its foundational concepts, which include rapport, sensory acuity, calibration, submodalities, and anchoring. These tools are essential for anyone seeking to become a master communicator and influencer, especially in high-stakes environments like the courtroom. In this section, we'll explore these concepts in depth, with a focus on practical applications for trial lawyering, negotiations, and witness management.

Building Bridges: Rapport as the Foundation of Connection

Rapport: The Secret to Effortless Influence

Rapport is the foundation of all successful communication. It's the ability to create a sense of trust, understanding, and connection with another person. In NLP, rapport is established by subtly mirroring and matching someone's behaviors, language, and attitudes, making them feel understood and comfortable. Think of rapport as the "bridge" that connects you to another person's world, allowing for seamless communication and influence.

In the legal field, rapport is critical. Whether you're working with a judge, a witness, or a jury, creating rapport ensures that your message is received openly. Without rapport, even the most compelling argument may fall flat, as the listener's defenses remain up.

The Attorney Who Mastered Rapport

Consider a young attorney named Sarah who struggled with her closing arguments. Despite having strong evidence, she often felt that the jury wasn't fully engaged. She decided to study rapport-building techniques from NLP, learning to mirror the body language and speech patterns of her audience. The next time she presented a case, she noticed subtle shifts—when she leaned forward, so did the jury members. When she spoke slowly and paused, they seemed to nod in sync. By the end of her argument, she had their full attention, and she won the case.

This demonstrates the power of rapport; it's the invisible thread that binds people together, allowing for influence without force.

Step-by-Step Guide: Establishing Rapport in Legal Settings

1. **Observe and Match Posture and Gestures**:
   - Pay close attention to the person's body language. Are they sitting upright or leaning forward? Are their hands crossed or open?
   - Subtly match their posture for a brief moment to create an unconscious sense of familiarity.
2. **Mirror Speech Patterns and Tone**:
   - Listen to the pace and tone of their voice. If they speak softly and slowly, do the same. If they are more animated, match their energy.
   - Gradually introduce your own pace or tone, leading them into a state where they are more receptive to your message.

3. **Use Similar Language**:
   o Pay attention to the specific words or phrases they use, and incorporate them into your response. If a witness says, "I felt uneasy," respond with, "I understand that uneasy feeling."

By practicing these steps, you establish rapport, making it easier to influence and guide the interaction toward your desired outcome.

Fine-Tuning Perception: Sensory Acuity and Calibration

Sensory Acuity: The Art of Noticing the Unseen

Sensory acuity is the ability to observe and detect subtle, often unconscious, changes in another person's physiology and behavior. It involves paying close attention to micro-expressions, shifts in breathing, skin tone, and muscle tension. In NLP, these subtle cues are seen as indicators of a person's emotional state and openness to influence.

Imagine you're cross-examining a witness. As you ask a critical question, you notice a brief hesitation and a slight shift in their posture. Their breathing quickens, and they glance down momentarily. These tiny signals—only visible through keen sensory acuity—indicate discomfort or uncertainty, providing a clue that you've touched on something important.

Calibration: Adjusting Your Approach in Real-Time

Calibration is the skill of adapting your behavior based on the feedback you receive from sensory acuity. It's a dynamic process, where you adjust your tone, posture, or questioning style to either amplify a reaction or diffuse tension. In trial lawyering, calibration is vital for managing interactions with witnesses, jurors, and judges.

For example, during a motion hearing, if the judge shows signs of disinterest or impatience (e.g., leaning back, crossing arms), you might need to adjust your delivery. By shifting your tone to one of urgency or using concise language, you recalibrate the interaction to regain their attention.

Advanced Technique: Using Sensory Acuity and Calibration in Jury Trials

1. **Observe Jury Reactions**: As you present evidence, look for micro-expressions—such as raised eyebrows, nods, or frowns—that indicate jurors' engagement levels.
2. **Calibrate Delivery Based on Feedback**: If you notice positive signals (e.g., nodding), amplify these with reinforcing statements like, "As you clearly understand..." If you see disengagement, change your pace, use visual aids, or ask rhetorical questions to re-engage them.
3. **Adapt Questioning During Cross-Examination**: If a witness exhibits discomfort, shift your posture to appear less confrontational or adjust your tone to be more supportive, making them more likely to open up.

Mastering sensory acuity and calibration allows you to remain flexible and adaptive, ensuring you maintain control over the direction and outcome of your interactions.

Submodalities: The Details That Shape Perception

Understanding Submodalities: The Building Blocks of Experience

In NLP, submodalities refer to the finer distinctions within each sensory experience that shape how we perceive and respond to the world. For example, when someone recalls a memory, they may experience it as a picture—this picture can vary in brightness, size, or color. Auditory experiences may differ in volume, pitch, or distance. By identifying and adjusting these submodalities, you can change how a person experiences and reacts to a particular thought or memory.

In the courtroom, this concept is incredibly useful. If you can guide a juror to imagine a piece of evidence as vivid, close-up, and detailed, they are likely to engage with it more intensely. Conversely, if you want to diminish the impact of the opposing counsel's point, you might encourage the jury to visualize it as small, distant, or faded.

Practical Application: Using Submodalities to Influence Perception in Closing Arguments

1. **Shift Visual Submodalities**: As you describe a key piece of evidence, ask the jury to "imagine it clearly, as if it were right in front of you—sharp, bright, and undeniable." This engages their visual submodalities, making the information more compelling.
2. **Adjust Auditory Submodalities**: When recounting a critical statement made by a witness, say, "Hear their words echoing clearly, the truth ringing out." By emphasizing the sound's clarity and volume, you amplify its impact.
3. **Change Kinesthetic Submodalities**: To evoke an emotional response, invite the jurors to "feel the tension in the air, as if they could almost reach out and touch the fear." This engages their physical sense, anchoring the emotion to your narrative.

By mastering submodalities, you can control how information is received and interpreted, giving you a powerful tool to influence outcomes.

Anchoring: Creating and Accessing Emotional States on Demand

Anchoring: The Key to Recalling Powerful States

Anchoring is one of NLP's most powerful tools, allowing individuals to associate a specific stimulus (such as a gesture, touch, or phrase) with a particular emotional or psychological state. This association makes it possible to access and trigger that state instantly when needed. In legal practice, anchoring can be used to maintain confidence, assertiveness, or calm during high-pressure situations like trials, negotiations, or when interacting with witnesses and jurors.

Imagine a lawyer named Tom who struggles with confidence during cross-examinations. He learns the technique of anchoring and decides to create an anchor for confidence. During practice sessions, he vividly recalls moments when he felt confident, imagining the sights, sounds, and sensations of those experiences. He then pairs this feeling with a simple gesture—pressing his thumb and forefinger together. With repeated practice, this gesture becomes an anchor for confidence, allowing him to access that state during trials, no matter how stressful the situation.

Step-by-Step Guide: Creating an Anchor for Confidence

1. **Choose a Positive Experience**: Find a moment in your past where you felt incredibly confident. Close your eyes and immerse yourself in that memory. Notice what you saw, heard, and felt at that moment.
2. **Intensify the Experience**: As you recall the memory, make the image brighter, the sounds clearer, and the feelings stronger. Make the memory as vivid as possible to heighten the state of confidence.

3. **Select a Unique Gesture**: Choose a simple and subtle gesture, like pressing your thumb and forefinger together or tapping your knee. Ensure that this gesture is something you can easily and discreetly use in a professional setting.
4. **Link the Gesture to the State**: At the peak of your emotional state—when the feelings of confidence are at their strongest—perform the chosen gesture. Repeat this several times, linking the gesture with the emotion.
5. **Test the Anchor**: After practicing, test the anchor by performing the gesture outside of the memory recall. Notice if the confident state returns. With practice, the state will become anchored and accessible whenever you need it.

Practical Applications of Anchoring in Legal Settings

1. Trials and Cross-Examinations

- **Maintaining Composure**: Before approaching the witness stand for cross-examination, use your anchor to access a state of calm and confidence. This will ensure you maintain control of your demeanor and delivery, even if the witness becomes uncooperative or hostile.
- **Amplifying Assertiveness**: When delivering key points during cross-examination, use your anchor just before speaking. This boosts your assertiveness, helping you to project authority and maintain dominance over the interaction.

2. Motion Hearings and Calendar Negotiations

- **Using Anchors for Persuasion**: In calendar negotiations with a DA or when arguing a motion before a judge, use an anchor to access a state of focus and assertiveness. This ensures that you present your points with clarity and confidence, increasing your persuasive power.

- **Calming Nerves**: If a judge challenges your argument or seems disinterested, accessing an anchor for calmness can help you stay composed and adjust your delivery to regain their attention.

The Power of Key NLP Concepts in Legal Practice

The foundational concepts of NLP—rapport, sensory acuity, calibration, submodalities, and anchoring—equip legal professionals with tools to influence, persuade, and communicate effectively in high-pressure environments. By mastering these techniques, attorneys can adapt to any situation, ensuring that they remain in control of interactions, whether with jurors, witnesses, judges, or opposing counsel. Each concept, when practiced and applied, enhances an attorney's ability to connect with others, read subtle cues, and influence outcomes in ways that feel seamless and effortless.

Through continued practice and application of these NLP principles, you can build the skills needed to excel in any legal setting, making you a more effective, adaptable, and confident communicator.

Applications of NLP in Law: Mastering Influence and Communication in the Courtroom

The application of Neuro-Linguistic Programming (NLP) techniques in the legal field is a transformative approach for attorneys who seek to elevate their influence, communication, and persuasive abilities. By adapting NLP strategies specifically for courtroom dynamics and legal negotiations, attorneys can better understand and guide the perceptions of jurors, witnesses, District Attorneys (DAs), and judges. This section delves into these applications, providing step-by-step instructions, practical scripts, and nuanced strategies for enhancing your effectiveness as a legal professional.

Adapting NLP Techniques for the Courtroom: Turning Theory into Persuasive Practice

The Courtroom as a Stage: Crafting Impactful Interactions

The courtroom is more than a place for legal proceedings—it's a stage where every word, gesture, and piece of evidence contributes to the narrative being presented. To become an effective communicator in this environment, attorneys must craft their delivery with precision and intent, ensuring that each element resonates with the jury, persuades the judge, and engages witnesses. NLP provides a toolkit for doing exactly this by leveraging body language, language patterns, and rapport-building techniques.

The Trial Lawyer Who Transformed Her Practice

Consider an attorney named Lisa, who often found that despite her preparation, her arguments didn't land as effectively as she'd hoped. Determined to make a change, she studied NLP techniques and began integrating them into her trial preparation. She learned to identify the dominant representational systems (visual, auditory, or kinesthetic) of jurors, subtly adjusted her language and gestures, and built rapport with witnesses using mirroring techniques. In her next trial, she noticed a remarkable difference—the jury seemed more engaged, the judge more attentive, and her cross-examinations more effective. She won the case with confidence, realizing that NLP had given her the edge she needed.

Understanding Jurors: The Key to Crafting Compelling Arguments

How Jurors Perceive Information: Identifying Representational Systems

Jurors, like everyone else, process information through their dominant representational systems—visual, auditory, or kinesthetic. Identifying these systems allows an attorney to adapt their communication style, ensuring the message is tailored to resonate with each juror's internal processing preferences.

Step-by-Step Guide: Tailoring Your Arguments to Jurors' Representational Systems

1. **Observe Jury Reactions During Voir Dire**:
   - Pay close attention to the language jurors use when answering questions. Visual jurors may say, "I see your point"; auditory jurors may respond with, "That sounds right"; kinesthetic jurors might say, "That feels fair."
   - Take note of body language—visual individuals may have more animated expressions, auditory people might tilt their heads when listening, and kinesthetic jurors may appear more grounded or tactile.
2. **Craft Your Argument Accordingly**:
   - For **visual jurors**, use imagery-rich language: "Picture the scene as it unfolded..." and present visual aids like diagrams, photos, or exhibits.
   - For **auditory jurors**, emphasize tone, clarity, and repetition: "Listen closely to the witness's words...," and vary your speech rhythm to maintain their attention.
   - For **kinesthetic jurors**, engage their emotions and physical sense: "Imagine how that must have felt, the weight of the moment..." and create

24

a narrative that evokes physical or emotional sensations.

3. **Engage All Systems in Closing Arguments**:
   - Integrate visual, auditory, and kinesthetic elements to ensure your argument reaches every juror. For example, "Picture the scene, listen to the facts again, and feel the impact of what happened."

By observing, adapting, and delivering arguments in ways that match jurors' representational systems, you maximize your chances of influencing the entire jury.

Practical Application: Influencing Jurors During Deliberation

Attorneys can also use NLP techniques to influence how jurors will recall and discuss information during deliberation. By anchoring specific words or gestures during key moments, an attorney can subtly guide jurors' perceptions and memories.

- **Example Script for Anchoring a Key Point**:
  - During closing arguments, say: "Remember the moment when the witness clearly stated...," while using a specific gesture like placing your hand on your chest. This gesture becomes an anchor, helping jurors recall your emphasis during their deliberation.

Witness Examination: Gaining Control with NLP Techniques

Building Rapport and Trust with Witnesses

Effective witness examination relies on establishing rapport, ensuring that witnesses feel comfortable and open, especially during direct examination. By mirroring their posture, tone, and language, you create an environment where witnesses are more likely to cooperate and provide valuable testimony.

Step-by-Step Guide: Rapport Techniques for Direct Examination

1. **Match the Witness's Posture and Tone**:
   - Start by subtly matching the witness's posture (e.g., if they sit upright, do the same). Use a similar tone when asking your initial questions to establish a connection.
2. **Use Supportive Language**:
   - Reinforce their responses with phrases like, "I appreciate you sharing that" or "Take your time, I understand this is difficult."
3. **Lead Them to Key Points**:
   - Once rapport is established, guide the witness to elaborate on critical facts with questions like, "Can you tell us more about what happened next?" while shifting your posture to lead their focus.

Cross-Examination: Using Sensory Acuity and Calibration

During cross-examination, NLP's sensory acuity and calibration techniques are crucial. They enable an attorney to detect shifts in the witness's state—such as discomfort or hesitation—and adjust their approach accordingly.

- **Calibration Technique for Witness Control**:
   - As you question the witness, observe their micro-expressions and breathing. If you sense tension, soften your tone or shift your body language to appear less confrontational.
   - If you notice openness or agreement, reinforce this state by leaning forward slightly and using affirmative language like, "Exactly, and that's why..."

Influencing Judges and DAs: NLP Techniques for Legal Negotiations

Calendar Negotiations: Finding Common Ground Through Rapport

Calendar negotiations with DAs often involve competing interests. Establishing rapport with the DA is essential to reach a mutually beneficial agreement. NLP techniques such as pacing, leading, and reframing objections are valuable tools in these negotiations.

Script for Effective Calendar Negotiations

- **Opening Line**: "I know we both have tight schedules, and I appreciate your willingness to work with me."
- **Pacing and Leading**:
  - Start by matching the DA's tone and pace. If they speak quickly, match their tempo briefly before gradually slowing down to create a sense of ease.
- **Reframe Objections**:
  - If the DA resists a proposed date, say: "I completely understand your concern about timing, but if we frame it as an opportunity to streamline the process for both of us, it might work out."

By building rapport, pacing the interaction, and reframing objections, you increase your ability to find common ground and negotiate effectively.

Motion Hearings: Persuading the Judge with Precision and Rapport

In motion hearings, NLP techniques can enhance your ability to persuade judges by building rapport and tailoring your arguments to their communication style. Judges, like everyone else, have their own preferences for processing information, and an attorney who adapts their approach gains a persuasive edge.

Step-by-Step Approach: Tailoring Arguments for Judges

1. **Identify the Judge's Preferences**:
   - Pay attention to how the judge responds to other attorneys. Do they prefer concise, direct arguments (auditory)? Are they more visual, relying on written briefs and diagrams? Or do they lean towards kinesthetic cues, focusing on the emotional or practical impacts of decisions?
2. **Adapt Your Delivery**:
   - For a judge who responds well to visuals, integrate charts or concise slides into your presentation.
   - For an auditory-oriented judge, emphasize clarity in your verbal delivery, using pauses and emphasis to highlight key points.
   - For a kinesthetic judge, focus on the implications and practical outcomes of your argument: "This decision ensures a fair process for everyone involved."
3. **Use Rapport Techniques to Build Trust**:
   - Begin with a tone and pace that matches the judge's demeanor. If they lean forward when listening, do the same when presenting your argument. This subtle mirroring establishes trust and connection.

The Strategic Advantage of NLP in Legal Practice

By adapting NLP techniques for the courtroom and legal negotiations, attorneys can influence and engage effectively with jurors, witnesses, judges, and DAs. Understanding how each group perceives information and tailoring communication strategies accordingly allows attorneys to present their cases more persuasively. Whether it's building rapport with a jury, managing a witness's state during examination, or negotiating with opposing counsel, NLP's tools provide a strategic advantage that enhances every aspect of legal practice.

Through consistent practice and application of these methods, attorneys can transform their influence, communication, and overall effectiveness, ensuring that their arguments are not just heard but felt and understood deeply by all parties involved.

As we move deeper into the realm of NLP applications in the legal field, it's essential to master the art of building rapport and influencing others. This next section focuses on specific techniques that establish trust and connection, allowing attorneys to effectively engage with judges, jurors, witnesses, and opposing counsel. By exploring methods such as mirroring and matching physical and verbal cues, as well as the strategic use of pacing and leading, lawyers can cultivate a sense of familiarity and trust with others. These foundational skills are crucial not only for developing effective non-verbal communication with jurors but also for building trust and openness with witnesses. By honing these abilities, attorneys gain the tools necessary to connect on a deeper level, increasing their persuasive power and enhancing their overall effectiveness in the courtroom.

2. The Art of Connection: Building Rapport and Influencing Others in the Courtroom"

In the high-stakes environment of the courtroom, the ability to build rapport and influence others is a critical skill that sets successful attorneys apart. Establishing a genuine connection with jurors, witnesses, judges, and opposing counsel goes beyond presenting evidence; it involves understanding and mirroring the subtle cues that create trust and credibility. In this section, we explore key techniques for developing rapport through mirroring and matching body language, tone, and pace, as well as using pacing and leading to guide interactions once rapport is established. We will also delve into the specifics of non-verbal communication with jurors, highlighting how eye contact, gestures, and facial expressions can foster a sense of connection. Finally, we examine the importance of building trust with witnesses, creating an environment where they feel comfortable and open, which is essential for eliciting honest and impactful testimony. Mastering these techniques allows attorneys to shape perceptions, enhance persuasion, and engage with every individual in the courtroom on a deeper, more influential level.

Building Rapport and Influencing Others: The Cornerstone of Persuasion

Rapport is the foundation of influence. By building a connection with another person, you create an environment where communication flows freely, trust is established, and influence becomes effortless. In legal practice, where the stakes are high and every interaction matters, mastering the techniques of building rapport is critical. This section explores how to effectively use mirroring and matching techniques, both physically and verbally, to establish this essential connection.

Mirroring and Matching Techniques: Reflecting the Path to Rapport

Mirroring and matching are powerful NLP techniques that allow an attorney to build rapport quickly and subtly. By reflecting someone's body language, gestures, and speech patterns, you create a sense of familiarity and understanding. People naturally feel comfortable around those who are like them, and when they sense this similarity, they are more likely to be open, trusting, and receptive.

Reflecting the Body: Physical Mirroring

The Subtle Art of Mirroring Body Language

Physical mirroring involves subtly copying another person's body language, gestures, and posture. This technique works because people unconsciously associate similarity with safety and trust. When someone sees their behavior reflected, they feel understood and more comfortable, even if they are unaware of it.

Imagine you are in a courtroom interacting with a judge. You notice that the judge leans back slightly and crosses their hands on the desk. By mirroring this posture—leaning back and resting your hands in a similar way—you create a subconscious bond. The judge feels an unspoken sense of rapport, which can make them more receptive to your arguments.

The Lawyer Who Mastered Physical Mirroring

Consider an attorney named Mark who struggled to engage jurors during trial. He often noticed jurors appearing disinterested or disengaged, even when he presented compelling evidence. Determined to change his approach, Mark learned about physical mirroring. He began to observe the jurors more closely, picking up on their subtle gestures and posture. If a juror leaned forward, he mirrored this movement as he spoke. If a juror crossed their arms, he mirrored it briefly before gradually opening his own posture, inviting them to do the same. Over time, Mark noticed a shift—the jurors seemed more attentive, nodding along as he spoke. By the end of the trial, he had gained their trust, and his client won the case.

This story illustrates the power of physical mirroring; it's not about copying others but reflecting their behavior in a subtle and respectful manner, fostering connection and understanding.

Step-by-Step Guide: Mastering Physical Mirroring in Legal Interactions

1. **Observe Body Language Carefully**:
   o Take a moment to assess the other person's posture, gestures, and movements. Are they leaning forward, sitting upright, or crossing their arms?
   o Pay attention to facial expressions—are they relaxed, tense, or neutral?
2. **Subtly Mirror the Behavior**:
   o Begin by mirroring their posture. If they lean forward, do the same. If they have their hands folded, mirror this position for a brief moment.
   o Avoid being too obvious; the mirroring should be subtle and natural, not forced.
3. **Gradually Lead the Interaction**:
   o Once rapport is established, gradually shift your posture to a more open and inviting stance. Often, the other person will unconsciously follow this lead, mirroring your openness.
   o This technique can be especially effective during witness examination, where creating a relaxed

environment encourages witnesses to share more freely.

Practical Application: Physical Mirroring in Various Legal Scenarios

1. **During Voir Dire (Jury Selection)**:
   o Observe jurors' seating positions and body language. If several jurors are sitting back with crossed arms, start by mirroring this posture briefly, then transition to an open posture to invite openness in return.
2. **In Calendar Negotiations with a DA**:
   o If the DA is sitting upright with a firm posture, mirror this at first to establish seriousness and mutual respect. Then, as the conversation progresses, shift to a more relaxed stance, signaling cooperation and flexibility.
3. **In Motion Hearings Before a Judge**:
   o Judges often have a neutral or authoritative posture. Begin by matching their posture to establish rapport, then gradually shift to a more open and engaged position when making your key arguments, inviting the judge to engage more attentively.

Echoing the Words: Verbal Mirroring

The Language of Influence: Mirroring Tone, Pace, and Choice of Words

Verbal mirroring involves matching the tone, pace, and specific language of the person you are communicating with. This technique helps create an instant sense of understanding and alignment. By speaking their "language," you make the person feel heard and valued, enhancing the connection and increasing the likelihood that they will respond positively to your message.

For example, when communicating with a witness who speaks slowly and thoughtfully, matching this pace shows respect and understanding. If you suddenly speak quickly and in a high pitch, it may disrupt the connection, making the witness feel uneasy. By mirroring their pace and tone, you build rapport and create a space where they feel comfortable sharing their testimony.

The Attorney Who Mastered Verbal Mirroring

Meet Laura, a defense attorney known for her skillful cross-examinations. Laura used to struggle with witnesses who were uncooperative or defensive. She realized that her approach was too direct and sometimes clashed with the witness's communication style. Determined to improve, she started using verbal mirroring techniques.

When she encountered a hesitant witness, she matched their slower pace and softer tone, echoing their choice of words. If a witness said, "I'm not entirely sure," she would respond with, "I understand, and it's okay not to be entirely sure—just tell us what you remember." This approach put the witness at ease, and over time, they opened up more freely. Laura's success rate improved significantly as she learned to adapt her style to each individual witness.

This story highlights the importance of verbal mirroring—by adjusting your speech patterns to align with the other person, you create a bridge of understanding and trust.

Step-by-Step Guide: Implementing Verbal Mirroring in Legal Interactions

1. **Listen Carefully to Their Tone and Pace**:
   - Focus on whether the person speaks quickly or slowly, loudly or softly. Do they emphasize certain words or speak with a flat tone?
   - Notice their choice of words—do they use formal language or more casual expressions?

34

2. **Match Their Communication Style**:
   o Start by matching their pace and tone. If they speak slowly, slow down your speech to align with theirs. If they use a calm, low tone, mirror this.
   o Use similar language and terminology. If they use specific phrases, incorporate these into your response. For example, if they say, "I just want to clarify," respond with, "I appreciate that you want to clarify."
3. **Gradually Guide the Conversation**:
   o Once you've established rapport through mirroring, you can begin to lead the conversation. If you need to pick up the pace, do so gradually, bringing the other person along with you.
   o This approach is particularly useful when negotiating with a DA or during motion hearings when you need to guide the flow of conversation while maintaining rapport.

Practical Application: Verbal Mirroring Across Legal Scenarios

1. **Engaging Jurors During Opening Statements**:
   o Pay attention to the overall energy and reactions of the jury. If they appear alert and engaged, speak with enthusiasm. If they seem hesitant, mirror a calm, steady tone, gradually building intensity as you deliver your argument.
2. **Witness Examination**:
   o For a cooperative witness, match their language patterns and phrases, affirming their statements and reinforcing the rapport you've established. For example, if they say, "I was trying to recall," you might respond with, "Take your time, I understand it's important to recall accurately."
   o If a witness seems defensive, begin by matching their tone and slowly transitioning to a more

supportive tone, guiding them into a state where they feel safe and open to share.

3. **Calendar Negotiations with Judges**:
   - When presenting your case for a scheduling change, match the judge's tone—if they are formal and direct, adopt a similar style. Gradually soften your tone to present your flexibility and cooperation, allowing the judge to feel in control while being subtly guided toward your preferred outcome.

The Power of Mirroring and Matching Techniques

Mastering the techniques of physical and verbal mirroring is essential for building rapport and influencing others effectively in the legal field. These strategies create a sense of connection and trust, making people more receptive to your message, whether you are engaging with jurors, questioning witnesses, negotiating with DAs, or addressing a judge.

By practicing and refining these techniques, attorneys can enhance their ability to influence outcomes in subtle yet powerful ways. This mastery not only improves communication but also elevates their effectiveness, ensuring they connect with others on a deep, influential level, no matter the setting.

Pacing and Leading: Guiding the Flow of Influence

Pacing and leading are advanced NLP techniques that build upon the foundational skills of mirroring and matching. By pacing someone's behavior, you create rapport and align yourself with their state, setting the stage for guiding or leading them toward your desired outcome. This technique is powerful in legal contexts, where attorneys must navigate delicate interactions, whether with jurors, witnesses, judges, or opposing counsel. Mastering pacing and leading allows attorneys to subtly influence these interactions, moving them toward their strategic objectives while maintaining trust and rapport.

The Power of Pacing: Aligning with the Other's Reality

Pacing: The Key to Establishing Trust and Rapport

Pacing involves aligning your behavior, language, and energy level with another person to create a sense of connection and trust. By mirroring their physical posture, tone, pace of speech, or emotional state, you demonstrate understanding and empathy, which makes the other person feel comfortable and open. The idea is that before you can influence someone, you must first "meet them where they are."

Imagine you are in a trial, presenting evidence to a jury. You notice that the jurors appear hesitant and uncertain. By pacing their energy—perhaps slowing your speech and adopting a calm, measured tone—you create a connection that mirrors their current state. This subtle alignment communicates that you understand their hesitation, setting the foundation for leading them toward the perspective you want them to adopt.

The Attorney Who Learned to Pace Before Leading

Consider an attorney named James, who often faced challenges when addressing judges in motion hearings. He would jump straight into his arguments with enthusiasm, only to find that some judges seemed disengaged or even irritated. Realizing this, James decided to incorporate pacing into his approach. The next time he faced a judge who appeared indifferent, he slowed his speech, matched the judge's body language by leaning back slightly, and adopted a serious, calm tone. The judge's demeanor softened, and James was able to gradually shift the tone of the interaction, gaining the judge's attention and eventually guiding the discussion in his favor.

This story illustrates that pacing is about adjusting to the other person's state to build rapport, creating a platform for influence.

Step-by-Step Guide: Establishing Rapport Through Pacing

1. **Observe and Assess the Other Person's State**:
   - Pay attention to physical cues like posture, breathing patterns, and gestures. Is the person sitting upright, leaning forward, or appearing relaxed?
   - Listen closely to their tone and speech patterns. Are they speaking quickly, slowly, in a soft or loud tone?
2. **Match Their Physical and Emotional State**:
   - Adjust your posture, breathing, and gestures to reflect theirs. If they are sitting back with arms crossed, match this posture briefly before gradually opening up.
   - Mirror their tone and pace. If they speak slowly and thoughtfully, respond in a similar manner.
3. **Maintain the Pace Until Rapport is Established**:
   - Continue pacing until you notice signs of rapport, such as a relaxed posture, nodding, or a shift in their body language that matches yours.
   - Only proceed to the leading stage when you sense that the connection has been firmly established.

Leading: Guiding Others Toward Your Desired Outcome

Taking the Next Step: Leading Once Rapport is Established

Once rapport has been built through pacing, leading allows you to subtly guide the other person's behavior, thoughts, or emotions toward a desired state or outcome. The idea is that once someone feels aligned with you, they are more likely to follow your lead. Leading involves making gradual changes in your behavior or communication style that the other person unconsciously follows, moving them closer to the state or perspective you want them to adopt.

For instance, during a calendar negotiation with a DA, you might initially pace their cautious, guarded demeanor by mirroring their tone and body language. As rapport is established, you can start leading by shifting your tone to a more cooperative and open stance, subtly guiding the DA toward a more collaborative discussion.

The Prosecutor Who Mastered Leading

Sarah, a prosecutor, often struggled during witness cross-examinations. Witnesses would become defensive or hesitant, making it difficult to get the information she needed. She learned to first pace the witness's state, matching their slower speech and leaning in when they spoke. Once the witness seemed comfortable, Sarah would gradually increase her energy and enthusiasm, encouraging the witness to open up and respond more confidently. By pacing and then leading, Sarah consistently transformed defensive witnesses into cooperative ones.

This story highlights that leading is about making small, deliberate adjustments once rapport is built, guiding others naturally and without resistance.

Step-by-Step Guide: Techniques for Leading After Pacing

1. **Make Small, Incremental Changes**:
   - Once you've paced and established rapport, begin making subtle shifts in your posture or tone. For example, if you've been sitting back with arms crossed, slowly open your arms and lean forward.
   - Gradually increase your energy level if appropriate, encouraging the other person to mirror your openness and engagement.
2. **Shift the Focus or Direction of the Conversation**:
   - Once rapport is in place, introduce new topics or steer the conversation toward your goal. For instance, during a motion hearing, if you've paced the judge's serious demeanor, you can shift your tone to one of urgency or emphasize cooperation to influence their decision-making.
3. **Use Positive Reinforcement to Reinforce the Shift**:
   - If the other person follows your lead, reinforce this behavior with positive feedback or affirmations, like nodding, smiling, or verbally acknowledging their agreement.

Practical Applications: Pacing and Leading Across Legal Contexts

1. Trial Lawyering: Engaging Jurors Through Pacing and Leading

- **Pacing Jurors' Energy**:
   - In a trial setting, observe the overall energy and mood of the jurors. If they appear hesitant or neutral, begin your opening statement with a calm, reflective tone that matches their state.
   - As you sense engagement building—evidenced by nods or attentive body language—begin to

increase your energy, using a more dynamic tone and gestures to lead them into a state of engagement.

- **Leading Jurors to a Conclusion**:
  - Once rapport is established, guide the jurors through your narrative, subtly emphasizing key points and encouraging them to agree with your perspective by reinforcing their subtle affirmations (like nods or engaged eye contact).

2. Motion Hearings: Pacing and Leading Judges

- **Pacing the Judge's State**:
  - During a motion hearing, if a judge appears reserved or skeptical, match their posture (e.g., leaning back) and mirror their tone (e.g., calm and measured) to create rapport.
  - As the hearing progresses, gradually shift to a more assertive tone when highlighting the strengths of your argument, leading the judge to consider your perspective more seriously.
- **Leading with Emphasis**:
  - Emphasize cooperation and common goals to lead the judge to a favorable outcome. Phrases like "I appreciate the court's attention to detail, and I believe this motion serves our mutual goal of ensuring justice" can effectively shift the tone and focus.

3. Calendar Negotiations with DAs: Building and Leading Cooperation

- **Pacing the Initial Discussion**:
  - Begin by matching the DA's guarded tone and energy level, acknowledging their constraints or challenges: "I understand how tight our schedules can get, and I appreciate you working with me."
  - Once rapport is built, shift to a more collaborative and open tone, suggesting solutions

and guiding the conversation toward mutually beneficial outcomes: "If we approach it this way, we might find a time that suits both of our schedules."

- **Subtly Leading Toward Agreement**:
  - Use leading questions that align with the DA's interests: "Wouldn't it be easier if we set this date, so it doesn't interfere with other cases you're handling?" By framing the shift in a way that benefits them, you increase the likelihood of cooperation.

The Strategic Power of Pacing and Leading

Pacing and leading are essential techniques for establishing and guiding interactions in legal practice. By aligning with others through pacing and subtly shifting their focus or behavior through leading, attorneys can create powerful, persuasive interactions that build rapport and drive desired outcomes. Whether addressing jurors, negotiating with DAs, examining witnesses, or presenting arguments before judges, mastering these techniques ensures that attorneys can connect, influence, and succeed in the courtroom and beyond.

Practicing these methods consistently will allow attorneys to fine-tune their approach, ensuring they are adaptable and influential in every interaction they face.

Establishing Non-Verbal Communication with Jurors: The Silent Language of Influence

Non-verbal communication is a powerful tool in the courtroom, especially when it comes to engaging and influencing jurors. Words alone are not enough to persuade; the way an attorney conveys information through eye contact, facial expressions, and subtle gestures can have a profound impact on how jurors perceive the case. By mastering non-verbal cues, attorneys can build rapport, create trust, and guide jurors' emotions and attention, making their arguments more persuasive and memorable. This section explores the techniques of using eye contact, facial expressions, and gestures, as well as understanding and adapting to jury body language for maximum influence.

Eye Contact: Establishing a Direct Line of Connection

The Power of the Gaze: Engaging Jurors with Eye Contact

Eye contact is one of the most effective ways to establish rapport and trust. When used correctly, it creates a personal connection that draws jurors into the attorney's narrative. It demonstrates confidence, sincerity, and attentiveness, which are critical for shaping a jury's perception of the attorney's credibility. Jurors who feel seen are more likely to engage with the case and respond favorably to the attorney's arguments.

Imagine an attorney delivering their opening statement. As they scan the room, they make brief but meaningful eye contact with each juror. This act of acknowledgment signals that each juror's role is important and valued, helping to foster a connection that goes beyond the spoken word. The jurors, in turn, feel included and are more likely to focus on the attorney's message.

The Defense Attorney Who Mastered the Art of Eye Contact

Emily, a defense attorney, struggled with engaging jurors during her opening statements. She felt they were often distracted or disinterested, making it difficult for her to gain their trust. Realizing the importance of eye contact, she practiced making intentional connections with jurors during her next trial. As she spoke, she paused briefly to make eye contact with each juror, holding their gaze for just a moment before moving on to the next. The change was immediate—jurors became more attentive, nodding along as she presented her case. By the end of the trial, Emily's client received a favorable verdict, and she understood the power of eye contact as a tool for building trust and engagement.

Step-by-Step Guide: Using Eye Contact to Build Rapport

1. **Scan the Jury During Opening and Closing Statements**:
   - Begin by slowly scanning the jury, making brief eye contact with each juror to create a sense of inclusion. This shows that you are addressing the entire group, not just a single person.
   - Hold each juror's gaze for 1-2 seconds—enough to establish a connection without making them uncomfortable or feeling singled out.
2. **Use Prolonged Eye Contact for Emphasis**:
   - When delivering key points, select a specific juror and maintain eye contact for slightly longer (2-3 seconds). This reinforces the importance of your statement, making it feel more personal and impactful.
   - Avoid shifting your gaze too rapidly, as this can appear nervous or insincere. Instead, maintain a steady and confident demeanor.
3. **Adapt Your Eye Contact Based on Juror Reactions**:
   - If a juror maintains eye contact and nods, continue engaging them throughout the trial as a sign they are receptive to your message.
   - If a juror avoids eye contact, try using softer, indirect gazes or look toward the general area rather than directly at them. This approach can build comfort gradually.

Facial Expressions: Conveying Emotion Without Words

The Silent Influence: Using Facial Expressions to Guide Juror Perceptions

Facial expressions communicate emotion and intent, often more effectively than words. They can signal sincerity, empathy, or seriousness, helping jurors to connect emotionally with the narrative. Jurors pick up on these cues, consciously or unconsciously, and form impressions about an attorney's credibility and authenticity based on them. A well-timed expression can reinforce the emotional tone of an argument, making it more persuasive and memorable.

Imagine you are delivering a closing argument about the emotional impact of a crime on the victim's family. A sincere, empathetic expression reinforces your words, demonstrating to the jurors that you are genuinely invested in the case's outcome and the people affected. This alignment between your words and expressions deepens their emotional engagement and makes your argument more compelling.

The Prosecutor Who Transformed His Facial Expression Technique

Thomas, a prosecutor, often found that his closing arguments lacked the emotional impact he desired. Even when discussing sensitive details, his expressions remained neutral. After studying NLP techniques, he began consciously aligning his facial expressions with the emotions he wanted to convey. When describing the victim's suffering, he adopted a look of genuine concern; when emphasizing the severity of the defendant's actions, his expression became serious and resolute. The jurors' reaction was immediate—they leaned in, nodded, and appeared emotionally moved. Thomas's transformation underscored the importance of using facial expressions to connect with jurors on an emotional level.

Step-by-Step Guide: Employing Facial Expressions Effectively

1. **Align Your Facial Expressions with the Emotional Tone of Your Argument**:
   o For empathetic moments, soften your expression by raising your eyebrows slightly and nodding gently. This conveys understanding and compassion.
   o For serious or impactful moments, furrow your brow and maintain a focused, intense gaze. This signals the importance and urgency of your message.
2. **Use Smiles Sparingly and Strategically**:
   o Smiling can create a sense of warmth and openness, but it must be used appropriately. Smile when building rapport or making light-hearted comments, but avoid smiling during serious discussions, as it can appear insincere or unprofessional.
3. **Adapt Your Expressions Based on Juror Feedback**:
   o If a juror responds positively to your expression, maintain that expression longer to reinforce the connection. If you notice a lack of response, adjust by intensifying or softening your expression depending on the situation.

Subtle Gestures: Reinforcing Your Message Without Words

Gestures That Guide: Enhancing Communication with Visual Cues

Subtle gestures serve as powerful reinforcements for verbal messages. Gestures like open palms, nods, or gentle hand movements can convey openness, confidence, and sincerity. When used strategically, these gestures become visual tools that emphasize key points, invite agreement, or indicate understanding. They provide jurors with visual anchors that help them follow and internalize the narrative.

For example, when presenting evidence, using an open-palm gesture as you describe each piece creates a visual anchor that guides jurors through the argument. This visual support makes the information easier to follow and remember, enhancing the overall impact.

The Attorney Who Mastered Subtle Gestures

Sarah, an experienced trial lawyer, was known for her ability to connect with jurors through non-verbal cues. She often used subtle gestures when explaining evidence, such as placing her hand over her heart when speaking of sincerity or using an open-palm gesture when inviting jurors to consider her point. These gestures created a visual representation of her words, making her arguments more engaging and memorable. Jurors frequently commented that they felt a stronger connection and were more persuaded by her presentations.

Step-by-Step Guide: Employing Gestures to Connect and Influence

1. **Use Open Palms to Signal Transparency and Trust**:
   - When addressing the jury, use open palms when explaining evidence or presenting key points. This gesture indicates honesty and openness, making jurors more likely to trust you.
2. **Employ Nods to Encourage Agreement**:
   - Subtle nods during moments of agreement or emphasis invite jurors to nod along, creating a subconscious sense of alignment and agreement.
3. **Adapt Gestures Based on Jurors' Body Language**:
   - If jurors appear closed off (e.g., arms crossed), use open gestures to encourage them to open up. Gradually transition from a closed stance to

a more open posture, signaling a cooperative and inclusive approach.

Reading and Adapting to Juror Body Language: The Feedback Loop

Understanding Juror Cues: Observing and Interpreting Body Language

Jurors' body language provides immediate feedback on their level of engagement, agreement, or skepticism. Jurors who lean forward, nod, or maintain eye contact are likely engaged, while those who cross their arms, look away, or shift frequently may be disengaged or resistant. Observing these cues allows attorneys to adjust their delivery and approach to re-engage and build rapport.

Step-by-Step Guide: Adapting to Juror Body Language

1. **Identify Engagement Signals**:
   o Look for jurors who lean in, nod, or make eye contact. These are positive signals indicating they are receptive. Continue engaging them with direct eye contact and inclusive gestures.
2. **Adjust for Disengagement Signals**:
   o If a juror crosses their arms or avoids eye contact, adjust your body language to open up and invite connection. Uncross your arms, lean slightly forward, and use open-palm gestures to encourage openness.
3. **Re-engage Through Narrative and Emphasis**:
   o If you sense disengagement, shift your approach by rephrasing your point or emphasizing a different aspect of the story. For example, "I understand if this feels challenging, but let's consider it from this angle..."

Mastering Non-Verbal Communication for Maximum Influence

Non-verbal communication is a powerful tool for influencing and engaging jurors. By mastering eye contact, facial expressions, gestures, and adapting to jurors' body language, attorneys can build rapport, create trust, and effectively guide jurors' perceptions and emotions throughout the trial. These techniques, when practiced and refined, ensure that every interaction is strategically aligned to maximize the attorney's influence, making the verbal argument more compelling and the overall courtroom presence more impactful.

Building Trust with Witnesses: Creating the Foundation for Honest Testimony

In the courtroom, the ability to establish trust with witnesses is critical for eliciting clear and truthful testimony. Whether during direct examination, where the witness needs to feel comfortable and open, or cross-examination, where establishing rapport can soften resistance, building trust is essential. This section explores the techniques for creating a comfortable environment and encouraging open, honest communication, ensuring that witnesses feel safe and supported throughout their testimony. By mastering these techniques, attorneys can maximize the credibility and impact of witness statements, influencing the jury's perception and understanding of the case.

Creating a Comfortable Environment: Setting the Stage for Open Communication

The Importance of Comfort: Making Witnesses Feel Safe

Witnesses may feel anxious or intimidated when taking the stand, especially in high-pressure trial environments. It's crucial to create an environment that feels safe and supportive, encouraging the witness to speak openly and confidently. When witnesses sense that they are in a non-judgmental space where their words are valued, they are more likely to provide honest and complete testimony.

Imagine you are preparing a witness for direct examination. You begin by setting a tone of warmth and understanding, using open body language and a calm tone of voice. You engage them in small talk before diving into the case details, helping them relax and feel more comfortable in your presence. By reducing their stress level, you increase the likelihood of receiving clear, straightforward responses.

The Prosecutor Who Transformed Witness Preparation

Anna, a prosecutor, often struggled with nervous witnesses who provided vague or incomplete answers. She realized that her approach was too direct, failing to put the witnesses at ease. Determined to change, she began incorporating techniques from NLP. Before any questioning, she engaged in casual conversation with the witness, using open body language and mirroring their tone and pace to build rapport. She also reassured them about the process, explaining each step in simple terms. The results were striking—witnesses became more relaxed, open, and forthcoming during their testimonies, significantly enhancing the credibility of her cases.

Step-by-Step Guide: Techniques for Creating a Comfortable Environment

1. **Start with Small Talk**:
   o Engage in casual conversation before diving into the case details. Ask about their day or discuss a neutral topic to reduce initial anxiety.
   o Use a warm tone and relaxed body language, such as leaning slightly forward and maintaining a soft smile. This demonstrates approachability and care.
2. **Explain the Process Clearly**:
   o Explain what to expect during their testimony, including the types of questions you'll ask and how they should respond if they don't know an answer. Emphasize that it's okay not to have every detail.
   o Reassure them that the courtroom is a safe space where their perspective is valued, helping to build their confidence.
3. **Mirror and Match Their State**:
   o Observe the witness's body language and emotional state. If they appear tense, mirror their posture briefly, then gradually shift to a more open stance, inviting them to do the same.
   o Match their tone and pace initially, then slowly lead them to a calmer state by adjusting your own behavior.

Practical Application: Creating a Comfortable Environment in Various Legal Scenarios

1. **Direct Examination**:
   o Begin by asking simple, non-threatening questions that allow the witness to settle into their testimony. Avoid diving directly into critical issues; instead, start with background information they are confident about.

2. **Cross-Examination**:
   - While cross-examination can be adversarial, it's important to create a space where the witness feels comfortable enough to engage rather than shut down. Begin with neutral questions and use a respectful, calm tone to avoid triggering defensiveness.
3. **Motion Hearings and Depositions**:
   - In pre-trial settings, where witnesses may feel less formal pressure but still experience anxiety, establish rapport through a calm, reassuring approach. Emphasize that the information they provide will be used to support the case and that their honesty is crucial.

Encouraging Open, Honest Communication: Techniques for Effective Examination

Building the Pathway to Openness: Establishing Rapport

Rapport is the foundation for honest communication during witness examination. When witnesses feel that the attorney understands and values their perspective, they are more likely to open up and provide honest, detailed answers. This is especially important during direct examination, where the attorney's goal is to create a narrative through the witness's testimony.

The Attorney Who Mastered Rapport with Reluctant Witnesses

David, a defense attorney, often struggled with witnesses who were hesitant or reluctant to fully engage during their testimonies. Realizing the need for a different approach, he began to focus on rapport-building. Before questioning, he acknowledged the witness's concerns and expressed appreciation for their cooperation. He used open-ended questions and a calm, understanding tone, making the witness feel heard and respected. The shift was profound—witnesses became more cooperative and forthcoming, offering the insights he needed to strengthen his case.

Step-by-Step Guide: Techniques for Encouraging Honest Communication

1. **Acknowledge and Validate the Witness's Feelings**:
   - Begin by recognizing the witness's potential anxiety or discomfort. Simple statements like, "I understand this might feel overwhelming, but I'm here to guide you," help to validate their feelings and establish rapport.
2. **Use Open-Ended Questions (On Direct-Examination)**:
   - Frame your questions in a way that invites expansive responses. Instead of asking, "Did you see what happened?" ask, "Can you describe what you observed in your own words?"
   - This approach encourages the witness to share their perspective more fully, making them feel that their account is valued.
3. **Maintain a Calm, Steady Tone Throughout the Examination**:
   - Avoid abrupt changes in tone or volume, which can startle the witness and break rapport. Consistency in tone creates a sense of stability and safety, encouraging openness.
4. **Provide Positive Reinforcement**:
   - When the witness provides useful information, acknowledge it with affirmative gestures (like nodding) or verbal affirmations such as, "Thank you for explaining that; it's very helpful." This builds their confidence and encourages them to share more.

Practical Application: Techniques for Effective Witness Examination

1. **Direct Examination**:
   - Frame questions to lead witnesses through their story in a logical, comfortable manner. Avoid confrontational language, and provide verbal reinforcement when they provide clear, detailed responses.
2. **Cross-Examination**:
   - Even in adversarial situations, maintaining a respectful tone and acknowledging the witness's answers, even if they contradict your position, can build rapport. This can lead to unexpected openness, revealing information that supports your case.
3. **Preparing Witnesses for Trial**:
   - In pre-trial settings, spend time coaching witnesses on the importance of being honest and specific. Emphasize that you are there to support them and guide them through the process. This builds trust and ensures that when they are on the stand, they feel confident in your partnership.

Adapting Techniques During Examination: Reading and Responding to Witness Cues

The Feedback Loop: Adjusting Techniques Based on Witness Reactions

During examination, witnesses provide non-verbal cues that indicate their comfort level and willingness to engage. An effective attorney must read these cues and adjust their approach accordingly to maintain or restore rapport. Signs of discomfort, such as avoiding eye contact, fidgeting, or crossing arms, indicate that the witness may be feeling defensive or anxious.

Step-by-Step Guide: Adapting Techniques During Examination

1. **Identify Signs of Discomfort**:
   - Watch for non-verbal signals like shifting posture, avoiding eye contact, or tightening facial expressions. These often indicate discomfort or resistance.
2. **Adjust Your Approach to Rebuild Rapport**:
   - If a witness shows signs of discomfort, slow your pace, soften your tone, and use open body language to signal support.
   - Shift from direct to more open-ended questions to give them the opportunity to respond comfortably.
3. **Encourage Engagement Through Positive Cues**:
   - If the witness shows signs of openness (e.g., leaning in, maintaining eye contact), continue using supportive language and gestures. This reinforcement strengthens the connection and encourages further openness.

Practical Application: Adaptive Techniques Across Legal Scenarios

1. **Jury Trials**:
   - When examining witnesses before a jury, it's crucial to maintain rapport to present credible, engaging testimony. Adjust your approach based on the witness's non-verbal cues, maintaining a steady connection that jurors can perceive as genuine.
2. **Motion Hearings**:
   - In non-jury settings, witness comfort remains vital. Judges also observe witness demeanor, and your ability to adapt ensures that the witness remains credible and consistent throughout questioning.

Mastering Witness Communication for Legal Success

Building trust with witnesses is a cornerstone of effective trial advocacy. By creating a comfortable environment, encouraging honest communication, and adapting techniques based on witness cues, attorneys can ensure that their witnesses provide clear, credible, and compelling testimony. These skills, when honed and practiced, enhance the attorney's ability to present a powerful case, connecting the witness's story to the jury's understanding in a way that is engaging, authentic, and persuasive.

As we move into the realm of language patterns and persuasion techniques, we explore the art of using words strategically to influence and shape perceptions in the courtroom. In this section, we delve into advanced NLP methods like the Milton Model, which employs hypnotic language patterns to bypass resistance and subtly embed suggestions, and the Meta Model, which focuses on precision language to challenge vague statements and extract details during cross-examination. Additionally, we examine framing and reframing techniques, powerful tools for shifting perspectives and altering the context or meaning of statements to present facts in a more favorable light. Finally, we explore chunking techniques, which allow attorneys to zoom in on specifics during witness questioning or generalize points for impactful closing arguments. These methods provide attorneys with a comprehensive toolkit for crafting persuasive communication, ensuring that every statement and question is strategically designed to influence the jury's perception and guide them toward a desired outcome.

3. Mastering the Art of Persuasion: Advanced Language Patterns and Techniques for the Courtroom

Language is a powerful tool for shaping perception, influencing decisions, and guiding narratives—especially in the courtroom, where the stakes are high and every word counts. This section delves into advanced NLP language patterns and persuasion techniques that equip attorneys with the ability to craft compelling communication strategies. From the Milton Model's hypnotic language patterns, designed to bypass resistance and subtly influence jurors and witnesses, to the Meta Model's precision questioning techniques that uncover crucial details during cross-examination, these methods are key to building persuasive arguments. We also explore framing and reframing techniques that allow attorneys to shift perspectives and recontextualize information for maximum impact, as well as chunking techniques that provide the flexibility to either hone in on specifics or generalize information for emphasis. Mastering these techniques ensures that attorneys can strategically guide the flow of information, present facts in a favorable light, and effectively influence the outcome of their cases.

The Milton Model: Hypnotic Language Patterns for Persuasion

The Milton Model, developed by Richard Bandler and John Grinder in the context of NLP, is a powerful set of hypnotic language patterns designed to influence and persuade by bypassing conscious resistance. Named after the renowned hypnotherapist Milton Erickson, the model uses vague and indirect language to access the subconscious mind, allowing attorneys to subtly embed suggestions and guide their audience's perception without triggering opposition. This technique is particularly valuable in the courtroom, where jurors, witnesses, and even judges may naturally resist overt persuasion attempts. By mastering the Milton Model, attorneys can communicate in ways that bypass these defenses, guiding their audience to adopt favorable perspectives and make decisions aligned with their arguments.

Using Vague Language to Bypass Resistance

The Art of Ambiguity: Influencing Without Opposition

One of the core principles of the Milton Model is using vague and ambiguous language. This strategy allows the listener's subconscious mind to fill in the gaps, making the message more personally relevant and less likely to be resisted. When people encounter vague language, they tend to interpret it in a way that aligns with their own experiences, emotions, or beliefs. This allows the speaker to guide the listener's thinking without triggering conscious objections.

Imagine you are addressing a jury. Instead of stating, "The defendant's actions were reckless and caused harm," which could trigger jurors to scrutinize or resist your statement, you say, "It's easy to see how some actions, without the right care, might lead to consequences none of us would want." This more ambiguous language invites the jurors to fill in the blanks themselves, aligning with the narrative you intend to build without presenting a direct challenge to their preconceptions.

The Attorney Who Mastered Vague Language

Consider a defense attorney named Rachel, who often struggled with jurors resisting her arguments. She realized that when she made direct, explicit statements, some jurors would immediately start questioning her credibility. Determined to change her approach, Rachel began practicing the Milton Model's vague language patterns. During a closing argument, instead of explicitly stating her client's innocence, she used phrases like, "Some people might see how a situation could unfold differently, considering all the factors." She noticed that jurors leaned in, appearing to contemplate her words more deeply. By the end of the trial, Rachel's client was acquitted, and she understood the power of subtle, indirect language in bypassing juror resistance.

Step-by-Step Guide: Using Vague Language to Influence

1. **Start with Ambiguous Phrases**:
   o Use phrases that suggest an idea without explicitly stating it. Examples include: "Some might wonder if...," "It's possible that...," or "Imagine if..."
   o This invites listeners to engage with the concept without feeling forced to accept a specific perspective.
2. **Allow the Listener's Imagination to Fill in the Gaps**:
   o Phrases like "You might already know..." or "There are those who might feel..." leave room for the listener to complete the thought, making it feel like their own.
3. **Use Generalizations That Can't Be Easily Disputed**:
   o General statements like "Sometimes things aren't as they seem" or "People often find that..." are difficult to argue against because they are universally relatable, making it easier to guide the listener's interpretation.
4. **Avoid Direct Challenges or Assertions**:
   o Instead of saying, "The witness is unreliable," you might say, "There are times when memories aren't as clear as we would hope." This approach is less confrontational and allows jurors to arrive at the intended conclusion without feeling pressured.

Practical Application: Vague Language in Legal Scenarios

1. **Trial Lawyering**:
   - During jury selection, use vague language to invite jurors to consider their biases without confronting them directly. For example, "Some of us might have certain feelings about these situations, and that's understandable."
   - In opening statements, frame your case with general, open-ended language that paints a picture without demanding agreement: "In a world where things happen so quickly, it's easy to see how events can be misunderstood."
2. **Calendar Negotiations with DAs**:
   - When negotiating schedules or plea deals, use vague language to create a sense of openness and collaboration. "I think there's room for us to explore options that work for both of us."
3. **Motion Hearings Before Judges**:
   - When presenting motions, use indirect language to subtly influence the judge's perception: "It may seem that, given the evidence, the outcome could lean in a certain direction."

Embedding Suggestions: The Power of Subtle Influence

Planting Seeds: Embedding Suggestions for Maximum Impact

Embedding suggestions within communication is a technique where you subtly influence the listener's thinking or behavior by hiding commands or ideas within a larger, seemingly neutral message. This approach is effective because it bypasses the listener's conscious defenses, allowing the suggestion to be processed subconsciously. It's akin to planting a seed that grows into a thought or feeling that aligns with your argument or desired outcome.

Imagine you're cross-examining a witness. Instead of directly suggesting they are unreliable, which may cause them to become defensive, you might say, "It's understandable that, in situations like this, people sometimes feel unsure about what they remember." This statement contains an embedded suggestion that implies doubt without explicitly accusing the witness. The subtlety allows the idea to sink in without triggering opposition.

The Attorney Who Embedded Suggestions for Success

Mark, a prosecutor, struggled during cross-examinations when witnesses became defensive. After learning the Milton Model, he began embedding suggestions into his questions. Instead of asking, "Did you forget what happened next?" he would say, "Sometimes, it's easy to overlook details when events unfold so quickly, isn't it?" The embedded suggestion allowed the witness to unconsciously align with the idea that forgetting details is natural, which reduced defensiveness and led to more honest responses. Mark's cross-examinations became far more effective, and he gained a reputation for his skillful questioning.

Step-by-Step Guide: Embedding Suggestions in Communication

1. **Use Pacing Statements to Set the Stage**:
    o Begin with statements that align with the listener's experience to create agreement, such as, "You've likely noticed that..." or "It's common for people to feel..."
    o This builds rapport and reduces resistance, making the listener more receptive to the embedded suggestion.

2. **Embed Commands or Suggestions Within a Larger Context**:
   - o Hide your suggestion within a broader statement: "As you consider all the details, you might find yourself understanding more clearly." The suggestion "understanding more clearly" is subtly planted within the statement.
3. **Use Softening Language to Reduce Resistance**:
   - o Words like "maybe," "perhaps," or "you might find" soften the embedded suggestion, making it less likely to trigger defensiveness. For example, "Perhaps you've already begun to see the connection."
4. **Frame Suggestions as Observations Rather Than Directives**:
   - o Instead of telling jurors or witnesses what to think, frame the suggestion as something they might notice themselves: "You may have already realized that..." or "Some people find that..."

Practical Application: Embedding Suggestions in Legal Scenarios

1. **Juror Interactions**:
   - o During opening and closing statements, embed suggestions that guide jurors' thinking without directly instructing them. For example, "As you hear the evidence, you might start to notice the pattern that's unfolding."
2. **Direct and Cross-Examinations**:
   - o Use embedded suggestions to guide witnesses into a particular frame of mind without confrontation. "In situations like these, people often find themselves unsure about exact details, wouldn't you agree?"
3. **Motion Hearings and Calendar Negotiations**:
   - o When addressing judges or DAs, embed suggestions that align with your desired outcome: "As we consider all the options, it's

easy to see why a swift resolution might benefit everyone involved."

Mastering the Milton Model for Persuasive Communication

The Milton Model's use of vague language and embedded suggestions is a powerful tool for influencing without triggering resistance. By creating a space where jurors, witnesses, or even judges can fill in the blanks and arrive at conclusions on their own, attorneys can subtly guide perceptions and decisions. Mastering these techniques ensures that every word and phrase is strategically crafted to build rapport, bypass defenses, and subtly shape the audience's thinking. With practice, these methods become a seamless part of communication, enhancing the attorney's effectiveness in trials, negotiations, and hearings, and ultimately influencing case outcomes in their favor.

The Meta Model: Precision Language for Clarity and Control

The Meta Model, developed by Richard Bandler and John Grinder, is a linguistic tool within NLP designed to bring clarity and precision to communication. It operates as a questioning framework, challenging vague or ambiguous statements to uncover the deeper, specific meaning behind them. By asking precise questions, attorneys can break down generalizations, distortions, or deletions in a witness's or opponent's language, revealing critical details and facts. Mastering the Meta Model is essential for trial lawyers, as it enables them to control the flow of information, guide witnesses toward clear and truthful testimony, and dismantle opposing arguments with precision.

Precision Questions: Turning Ambiguity into Clarity

From Ambiguity to Specificity: The Power of Precision Questions

In the courtroom, vague or ambiguous statements are common, especially when witnesses are nervous, evasive, or unsure of their memories. The Meta Model provides a structured approach for attorneys to challenge these statements, transforming them into specific, actionable information. Precision questions help attorneys drill down into the details, ensuring that jurors and judges receive the clearest and most accurate information possible.

Imagine a witness says, "I'm not sure, but I think I saw him there." This vague statement leaves room for ambiguity and doubt. An attorney using the Meta Model might respond, "What specifically made you think you saw him there?" or "What do you remember seeing?" These questions force the witness to access specific memories, reducing ambiguity and providing a clearer account of events.

The Attorney Who Used Precision Questions to Reveal the Truth

Lucas, a defense attorney, often found himself frustrated by witnesses who gave vague or noncommittal answers. One day, during a cross-examination, a witness said, "I don't really remember what happened." Rather than letting the statement stand, Lucas applied the Meta Model techniques he had practiced. He asked, "What part of it do you remember clearly?" and followed up with, "What happened just before you felt unclear?" The witness paused, then provided a detailed account of events leading up to the moment of uncertainty. Lucas's precision questions uncovered critical details that helped shift the jury's perception in his client's favor.

This story illustrates the power of the Meta Model in transforming vague statements into specific, useful information, demonstrating how precision questioning can turn the tide in a trial.

Step-by-Step Guide: Asking Precision Questions in Legal Contexts

1. **Identify Ambiguities, Generalizations, and Deletions**:
   - Listen carefully for vague statements, such as "I think," "probably," "some people say," or "I felt." These phrases often indicate that the speaker is generalizing, deleting information, or avoiding specifics.
2. **Use Specific Questions to Clarify and Challenge**:
   - Ask direct questions that target the ambiguous parts of the statement. Examples include:
     - "What specifically do you mean by that?"
     - "Who are you referring to when you say 'some people'?"
     - "How exactly did that happen?"
   - These questions force the speaker to provide details they might be omitting or generalizing.
3. **Focus on the Details of Time, Place, and Action**:
   - Questions that focus on specifics, such as "When did this happen?" or "Where were you when you saw this?" help anchor the witness's memory, guiding them to recall and provide precise information.
4. **Probe the Emotional Language**:
   - If a witness says, "I felt uneasy," respond with, "What specifically made you feel uneasy?" This not only clarifies the statement but also reveals the underlying facts that contributed to their feelings.

Practical Application: Precision Questions Across Legal Scenarios

1. **Trial Lawyering**:
   - During direct examination, use precision questions to guide witnesses in building a coherent, detailed narrative that leaves little room for doubt or misinterpretation.
   - In cross-examination, precision questions help dismantle vague statements from opposing witnesses, ensuring that only clear and specific information is presented to the jury.
2. **Calendar Negotiations with DAs**:
   - When negotiating, use precision questions to uncover the specifics of the DA's constraints or concerns. For example, "What specific cases are preventing this date from working for you?" helps clarify their position and allows you to propose viable alternatives.
3. **Motion Hearings Before Judges**:
   - When presenting arguments or rebutting opposing counsel, employ precision questioning to challenge vague legal claims: "What specific statute supports your argument?" or "Can you provide a specific example of how this precedent applies here?"

Techniques for Cross-Examining Witnesses: Probing for Details

The Art of Dissecting Statements: Meta Model Techniques in Cross-Examination

Cross-examination is one of the most critical aspects of trial lawyering, and the Meta Model's precision language techniques are particularly effective in this phase. By dissecting vague or evasive statements, attorneys can expose contradictions, clarify critical details, and reveal the truth.

The goal is to methodically guide the witness into providing the precise information needed to strengthen the case or undermine the opposition.

Imagine you are cross-examining a witness who says, "I think he might have been there." Instead of accepting this ambiguous statement, you ask, "When you say 'might have been there,' what makes you unsure?" By probing further, you force the witness to confront the uncertainty in their statement, leading them to either clarify their position or reveal inconsistencies.

The Cross-Examiner Who Turned Ambiguity into Advantage

Jessica, a prosecutor, knew that a witness's testimony could make or break her case. During a high-profile trial, a key witness provided vague answers like, "I'm pretty sure that's what I saw." Jessica, armed with the Meta Model, asked, "What do you mean by 'pretty sure'? What did you specifically see?" The witness, pressured to be more precise, eventually admitted that they hadn't actually seen the event but had heard about it from another source. Jessica's precision questioning exposed the flaw in the testimony, leading to a favorable outcome for her case.

This example highlights how the Meta Model can be used strategically in cross-examination to reveal the truth and disarm witnesses who rely on vague language.

Step-by-Step Guide: Techniques for Probing Details During Cross-Examination

1. **Target Vague Phrasing**:
   o Listen for phrases like "I think," "maybe," or "I felt like." These phrases often hide uncertainty or lack of clarity. Use questions such as:
      ▪ "What do you mean by 'you think'?"
      ▪ "What makes you say 'maybe'?"

- "How did you feel that way?"
    - This forces the witness to clarify their statement or admit their uncertainty.
2. **Break Down Generalizations**:
    - When a witness generalizes (e.g., "People were saying..." or "Everyone knew"), ask, "Who specifically said that?" or "Who is 'everyone'?" This removes the anonymity of generalizations and brings the statement into specific, verifiable territory.
3. **Clarify Deletions and Omissions**:
    - Witnesses may omit critical details either deliberately or out of nervousness. If a witness says, "He left the room," ask, "What happened right before he left?" or "Where did he go?" These questions force them to provide the missing pieces, giving a clearer picture of events.
4. **Probe Assumptions and Inferences**:
    - If a witness says, "It looked like he was angry," respond with, "What specifically did you observe that made you think he was angry?" This shifts the focus from the witness's interpretation to observable, concrete facts.

Practical Application: Cross-Examination Techniques Across Legal Scenarios

1. **Jury Trials**:
    - During cross-examination, precision questions are essential for discrediting vague or unreliable testimony. Asking questions that challenge generalizations or demand specifics allows you to expose contradictions or exaggerations in a witness's account.
2. **Motion Hearings**:
    - In motion hearings, precision questioning helps attorneys clarify ambiguous points made by the opposing side, ensuring that the judge has a

clear understanding of the facts before making a decision.

3. **Direct Examination Preparation**:
   o When preparing your own witnesses, use precision questions to ensure they provide detailed, clear responses that withstand scrutiny during cross-examination. Practice asking, "What exactly did you see?" and "How do you know that's what happened?"

Mastering the Meta Model for Effective Courtroom Communication

The Meta Model is a powerful tool for attorneys, enabling them to transform vague, ambiguous language into clear, specific information. By mastering precision questions, attorneys can control the flow of information, challenge vague statements, and guide witnesses and jurors toward clarity and truth. These techniques, when practiced and refined, enhance the attorney's effectiveness in trial lawyering, motion hearings, and negotiations, ensuring that every statement is precise, impactful, and persuasive.

Framing and Reframing Techniques: Shaping Perception and Meaning

Framing and reframing are powerful linguistic tools used in NLP to influence how information is perceived and interpreted. In the legal field, these techniques allow attorneys to present facts and statements in ways that align with their narrative, influencing the jury's or judge's understanding of the case. By adjusting the context or content of a statement, attorneys can shift the meaning, turning a seemingly unfavorable situation into an advantage or weakening the opposing counsel's argument. Mastering framing and reframing techniques provides attorneys with a flexible and dynamic approach to persuasion, enhancing their ability to control the narrative and guide the outcome of legal proceedings.

Context Reframing: Shifting Perspective for Maximum Impact

The Power of Context: Presenting Facts in a Favorable Light

Context reframing involves changing the situation or circumstances surrounding a fact or event to shift its meaning. The goal is to alter how the information is perceived, creating a more favorable interpretation that supports the attorney's narrative. By changing the context, attorneys can turn a perceived weakness into a strength or highlight aspects that may have otherwise gone unnoticed.

For example, if a witness testifies that a defendant was frequently in a certain area known for criminal activity, this fact could be damaging. An attorney skilled in context reframing might present the situation differently, stating that the defendant was there to support community efforts or to meet family members, providing a positive or neutral reason for their presence. This new context shifts the jury's perception, transforming what could have been seen as incriminating into something benign or even admirable.

The Defense Attorney Who Reframed the Context

John, a defense attorney, was handling a case where his client's presence at a crime scene was heavily emphasized by the prosecution. Rather than disputing the client's presence, John chose to reframe the context. He explained that his client was there because he regularly visited a nearby community center where he volunteered. John even called witnesses who could attest to his client's consistent involvement in community activities. This shift in context allowed the jury to see the client's presence as a sign of his commitment to helping others, rather than an indication of criminal behavior. The verdict was not guilty, demonstrating the power of effective context reframing.

Step-by-Step Guide: Applying Context Reframing in the Courtroom

1. **Identify the Existing Context**:
   - Determine the current perception of the event or fact. Ask yourself: How is the jury or judge currently interpreting this information? What assumptions are they making?
2. **Change the Context to Shift Perspective**:
   - Find an alternative context that aligns with your narrative. Consider different motives, circumstances, or reasons that could explain the fact in a way that supports your case.
   - For example, if a witness testifies that a client was seen with a suspicious item, reframe by stating, "In his profession, carrying tools like that is common practice."
3. **Present the New Context with Supporting Evidence**:
   - Provide evidence or testimony that reinforces the new context. This could include character witnesses, documents, or expert testimony that explains why the new interpretation is plausible.
4. **Invite the Jury or Judge to Consider the New Context**:
   - Use phrases like, "Imagine if..." or "Consider for a moment that..." to guide the audience into exploring the new perspective you're presenting. This encourages them to visualize the situation differently and become more receptive to your interpretation.

Practical Application: Context Reframing Across Legal Scenarios

1. **Direct Examination**:
   - During direct examination, use context reframing to present your witness's actions or statements in a way that highlights their integrity or innocence. For example, "My client was there because he was supporting his friend during a difficult time."
2. **Cross-Examination**:
   - If an opposing witness gives damaging testimony, reframe the context by suggesting alternative, non-threatening motives or circumstances. For example, "Isn't it possible that what you saw was just a friendly exchange, given their long history?"
3. **Motion Hearings**:
   - In motion hearings, frame the context of legal arguments to emphasize fairness and justice. For instance, "The defense's request for additional discovery isn't about delaying the trial; it's about ensuring that the truth comes out."

Content Reframing: Changing the Meaning of Statements

Transforming the Message: Altering the Interpretation of Information

Content reframing involves changing the meaning of a statement by adjusting its interpretation rather than the context. This technique focuses on the words themselves, providing a different perspective that shifts the overall message. Content reframing is especially useful when an opposing witness or attorney uses language that appears damaging. By altering how the information is understood, attorneys can reduce its impact or turn it to their advantage.

For example, if a witness describes the defendant as "confrontational," the term may initially seem negative. An attorney using content reframing might reinterpret it by saying, "Yes, he is assertive—he stands up for what he believes in." By shifting the meaning of "confrontational" to "assertive," the attorney changes the perception from negative to positive, supporting their client's character.

The Prosecutor Who Mastered Content Reframing

Emily, a prosecutor, encountered a witness who described her client's actions as "reckless." Rather than disputing the term, Emily reframed it by saying, "Yes, he acted quickly in a high-pressure situation—he made a decisive choice to protect others." The reframing shifted the meaning of "reckless" from carelessness to quick decision-making under pressure, which aligned with her narrative. The jury began to see the client's actions in a different light, ultimately leading to a successful conviction.

Step-by-Step Guide: Applying Content Reframing Techniques

1. **Identify the Negative or Ambiguous Statement**:
   o Pinpoint the specific word or phrase that carries a negative or ambiguous meaning. For instance, if a witness describes your client as "nervous," focus on that term.
2. **Find a Positive or Neutral Reinterpretation**:
   o Consider how the statement can be interpreted in a way that aligns with your narrative. For example, "nervous" could be reframed as "cautious" or "thoughtful."
3. **Rephrase the Statement with the New Meaning**:
   o Present the revised interpretation confidently. "What you saw as nervousness was actually

caution—my client was carefully assessing the situation to avoid any unnecessary risks."

4. **Back Up the Reframed Interpretation with Evidence**:
   o Reinforce the new meaning with evidence or testimony. If you reframe "nervous" as "cautious," bring up a past instance where the client's caution led to a positive outcome.

Practical Application: Content Reframing in Legal Scenarios

1. **Jury Trials**:
   o During opening statements, use content reframing to preemptively shift the meaning of potentially damaging evidence: "The prosecution might describe this as reckless, but you'll see that it was a calculated decision made under pressure."
2. **Witness Preparation**:
   o When preparing witnesses, help them understand how to frame their answers positively. If they feel defensive, coach them to use words that align with the desired narrative, such as replacing "defensive" with "protective."
3. **Motion Hearings and Negotiations**:
   o Reframe legal arguments presented by opposing counsel to show their requests as unreasonable or excessive. For example, "What they're asking for isn't transparency; it's an attempt to overreach beyond what's necessary for a fair trial."

Practical Scripts: Employing Framing and Reframing Techniques

1. **Reframing During Cross-Examination**:

- If an opposing witness describes an event in a negative light:
  - "You mentioned the defendant seemed angry—could it also be that he was just expressing frustration at a difficult situation, showing he cared deeply about the outcome?"

2. **Reframing Opening Statements**:
   - Anticipate the opposing counsel's narrative and reframe: "The prosecution may say this was an act of negligence, but the evidence will show it was a moment of quick thinking in an unpredictable situation."

3. **Reframing During Closing Arguments**:
   - Shift the meaning of the opposition's narrative: "The defense wants you to believe this was impulsive, but let's not mistake urgency for recklessness—it was a response rooted in responsibility."

Mastering Framing and Reframing for Persuasion

Framing and reframing techniques are essential tools for attorneys, allowing them to reshape the narrative and control how facts and statements are perceived. By mastering context and content reframing, attorneys can present information in ways that align with their objectives, ensuring that every fact is interpreted favorably and every statement supports their case. These skills, when practiced and applied strategically, provide attorneys with the flexibility to turn challenges into opportunities, guiding jurors and judges toward favorable conclusions and influencing case outcomes.

Chunking Techniques: Balancing Specificity and Generalization for Persuasive Communication

Chunking is an NLP technique that involves moving between different levels of information—either by getting more specific (chunking down) or by generalizing (chunking up). In the legal context, chunking techniques are invaluable, as they allow attorneys to strategically control the depth and focus of information depending on the situation. By chunking down, an attorney can extract specific details during witness questioning, revealing precise information that supports their case. Conversely, chunking up is useful for generalizing points and emphasizing broader themes during closing arguments, helping to reinforce a cohesive and persuasive narrative. Mastering chunking techniques ensures that attorneys can dynamically adjust their approach, maximizing clarity, impact, and persuasion in every aspect of trial lawyering.

Chunking Down: Delving into Specifics for Precision and Clarity

Breaking Down Information: Uncovering Details with Chunking Down

Chunking down involves moving from general information to specific details. This technique is particularly effective during witness questioning, as it allows attorneys to dissect vague or ambiguous statements, leading witnesses to provide clearer, more precise answers. By guiding witnesses to focus on specifics, attorneys can build a more detailed and accurate narrative that supports their argument.

Imagine a witness says, "He was acting strangely." While this statement offers a general idea, it lacks specificity. An attorney using chunking down might ask, "What specifically did you observe that made you think he was acting strangely?" By breaking down the statement, the attorney prompts the witness to provide concrete details—such as gestures, expressions, or actions—that clarify the testimony.

The Attorney Who Used Chunking Down to Reveal the Truth

Sophia, a prosecutor, often encountered witnesses who gave vague descriptions during testimony. During one trial, a witness stated, "I saw the defendant looking suspicious." Rather than accepting the statement as is, Sophia employed chunking down. She asked, "What specifically did you see that made you feel he looked suspicious?" The witness, after some hesitation, described how the defendant was pacing and frequently checking his phone while looking around nervously. This detailed account strengthened the prosecution's case by providing clear, observable actions that aligned with their narrative. The jury was able to visualize the defendant's behavior, which ultimately contributed to a conviction.

Step-by-Step Guide: Chunking Down in Witness Questioning

1. **Identify General or Ambiguous Statements**:
   - Listen for vague phrases like "acting strangely," "seemed off," or "looked suspicious." These statements often lack the specifics needed for clarity.
2. **Ask Questions That Focus on Specifics**:
   - Use questions such as:
     - "What exactly did you see?"
     - "How did they behave?"
     - "What were they wearing, and what were they doing at that moment?"

- These questions guide the witness to focus on concrete details that clarify their initial statement.
3. **Break Down Statements into Observable Elements**:
   - If a witness describes an emotion (e.g., "He seemed angry"), ask for observable behaviors: "What did you see or hear that made you believe he was angry?" This shifts the focus from interpretation to specific, verifiable actions.
4. **Build Upon the Details Provided**:
   - Once the witness offers specifics, continue to drill down: "When he was pacing, where was he looking?" or "What did he say when you noticed his tone changed?" This deepens the information, creating a more vivid and detailed picture.

Practical Application: Chunking Down Across Legal Scenarios

1. **Cross-Examination**:
   - Use chunking down to dissect vague or misleading statements from opposing witnesses. This method reveals inconsistencies or contradictions that can undermine the credibility of their testimony.
2. **Direct Examination**:
   - Guide your own witnesses through chunking down to create a comprehensive and detailed narrative. By extracting specific details, you build a stronger case that leaves little room for doubt.
3. **Depositions and Pre-Trial Interviews**:
   - Employ chunking down during depositions to uncover as much detail as possible. This ensures that, during the trial, you can reference precise information and anticipate how witnesses may respond to questioning.

Chunking Up: Generalizing for Emphasis and Persuasion

The Art of Abstraction: Using Chunking Up to Highlight Key Themes

While chunking down focuses on specifics, chunking up moves in the opposite direction, generalizing information to emphasize broader themes. This technique is particularly effective in closing arguments, where the goal is to connect specific evidence or witness testimony to a larger narrative. By abstracting details into general principles or themes, attorneys can create a cohesive and compelling argument that resonates with jurors on an emotional and logical level.

For example, after presenting various pieces of evidence showing a defendant's consistent behavior, an attorney might chunk up by saying, "This pattern isn't just about one or two incidents—it's about a repeated, consistent behavior that shows a disregard for the law." By chunking up, the attorney ties specific events into a broader narrative, reinforcing the overall message and ensuring it stays with the jury.

The Defense Attorney Who Used Chunking Up to Shift Perception

Michael, a defense attorney, faced a challenging case where the prosecution presented numerous small instances of his client's behavior as evidence of guilt. Rather than disputing each point individually, Michael used chunking up in his closing argument. He said, "What we see here isn't a series of criminal acts; we see a person struggling to make the best choices in difficult circumstances—a person trying to navigate life's challenges." By generalizing the details, Michael reframed the case from a series of isolated incidents into a larger story of human struggle, shifting the jury's perception. His client received a reduced sentence, showing the power of chunking up in persuasive communication.

Step-by-Step Guide: Chunking Up in Closing Arguments and Persuasive Speaking

1. **Identify Key Details or Patterns**:
   o Look for repeated behaviors, themes, or pieces of evidence that can be grouped together. For example, multiple instances of similar actions or behaviors that point to a larger trend.
2. **Abstract the Details into a General Principle or Theme**:
   o Frame the specifics into a broader statement: "This isn't just about one mistake; it's about a consistent effort to..." or "All these events point to a larger pattern of..."
   o This helps jurors see the bigger picture, connecting individual pieces of evidence to a unified narrative.
3. **Use Metaphors or Analogies to Reinforce the Generalization**:
   o Analogies can be powerful tools for chunking up: "Just like drops of water form a river, each piece of evidence contributes to a clear picture of intent."
   o Metaphors simplify complex details, making the message more relatable and memorable for the audience.
4. **Reinforce the Theme Throughout Your Argument**:
   o Return to the generalized theme multiple times during your argument: "As we've seen again and again, this pattern shows..." Repetition reinforces the narrative, ensuring it sticks with the jury.

Practical Application: Chunking Up Across Legal Scenarios

1. **Closing Arguments**:

- o Use chunking up to tie together witness testimonies, evidence, and expert opinions into a cohesive, overarching theme. This approach strengthens the emotional and logical appeal of your argument, making it more persuasive.

2. **Motion Hearings**:
   - o Frame legal principles in a generalized manner to highlight fairness and justice. For instance, "At its core, this motion is about ensuring that every defendant has the right to a fair trial."

3. **Calendar Negotiations and Plea Bargains**:
   - o When negotiating, generalize the benefits: "Agreeing to this schedule benefits both parties— it's about efficiency and finding a resolution that serves justice."

Practical Scripts: Employing Chunking Techniques

1. **Chunking Down During Cross-Examination**:
   - o If a witness says, "He was acting aggressively," follow up with:
     - "What did he specifically do that made you say that?"
     - "What exactly did you see or hear?"

2. **Chunking Up in Closing Arguments**:
   - o Generalize evidence into a broader theme:
     - "All these actions demonstrate a consistent disregard for safety, pointing to a clear pattern."
     - "This isn't just one isolated mistake; it's part of a larger series of actions that reflect a broader attitude."

3. **Chunking Up in Motion Hearings**:
   - o When advocating for a motion, generalize its importance:
     - "Granting this motion isn't just about this one case; it's about upholding the principle of fairness that the justice system relies on."

Mastering Chunking Techniques for Precision and Persuasion

Chunking techniques provide attorneys with the flexibility to navigate between specificity and generalization, adapting their approach based on the needs of the moment. By chunking down, attorneys extract crucial details that clarify and strengthen their case; by chunking up, they create persuasive, overarching themes that resonate with jurors and judges. Mastering these techniques ensures that attorneys can dynamically control the narrative, presenting information in ways that maximize clarity, impact, and influence, ultimately shaping the outcome of legal proceedings.

As we move into the realm of anchoring emotional states, we explore the powerful NLP technique of creating and triggering emotional anchors to influence behavior and responses. Anchoring is essential for attorneys seeking to manage their own emotional states under pressure, establish positive and confident testimonies from witnesses, and shape juror reactions. This section covers techniques for self-management, helping attorneys build and activate personal anchors for confidence, focus, and calm during trials. We also dive into methods for working with witnesses, establishing and triggering familiar positive states to enhance credibility and clarity during testimony. Lastly, we discuss how to use anchoring techniques with jurors, associating positive emotional states with key evidence and arguments while avoiding negative anchors that could lead to disengagement. Mastering these anchoring techniques provides attorneys with a versatile toolkit for managing emotions, influencing behavior, and strategically guiding courtroom dynamics.

4. Harnessing Emotional Anchors: Techniques for Influence and Control in the Courtroom

Emotional anchoring is a powerful tool within NLP that allows attorneys to create, trigger, and control emotional states in themselves, witnesses, and jurors. By establishing and activating emotional anchors, attorneys can maintain their own composure, confidence, and focus during high-pressure situations like trials, while also guiding witnesses into positive, calm states that enhance their credibility and testimony. Additionally, anchoring techniques enable attorneys to subtly influence juror reactions by associating positive emotions with key pieces of evidence, strengthening their impact. This section explores how to master these anchoring methods, from self-management to witness preparation and juror influence, providing practical strategies and applications for effectively navigating and controlling the emotional dynamics of the courtroom.

Anchoring Techniques for Self-Management: Building Emotional Resilience

Anchoring is a core NLP technique that involves associating a specific stimulus (such as a gesture, word, or touch) with a desired emotional state, allowing individuals to access that state whenever needed. For attorneys, mastering self-anchoring techniques is crucial for maintaining confidence, focus, and calmness, especially under the intense pressure of trial lawyering. By creating and effectively triggering these emotional anchors, attorneys can ensure they perform at their best, regardless of the challenges or high-stakes situations they face.

Creating Personal Anchors: Building Emotional States for Success

The Foundation of Emotional Anchors: Establishing Powerful Associations

To create a personal anchor, an attorney must associate a specific action, such as pressing two fingers together or taking a deep breath, with a powerful, positive emotional state like confidence, focus, or calmness. This process involves vividly recalling a past experience where the desired emotional state was at its peak and linking it to a chosen physical action or gesture. The key is to practice this consistently, so the brain begins to associate the gesture with the emotional state, making it accessible on demand.

Imagine a trial attorney who frequently experiences anxiety during opening statements. To build an anchor for confidence, they vividly recall a moment when they felt absolutely certain of their abilities—perhaps when they successfully argued a difficult motion or received a favorable verdict. As they immerse themselves in this memory, they press their thumb and index finger together, repeating this process several times to cement the association. Over time, this gesture becomes a trigger for confidence, allowing the attorney to access that emotional state whenever they feel nervous.

The Attorney Who Built Anchors for Confidence

Meet Alex, a defense attorney known for his strong casework but often plagued by self-doubt during high-pressure moments like cross-examinations. Determined to overcome this, Alex decided to create an anchor for confidence. He remembered the moment he won his first case—a powerful memory where he felt unstoppable. He closed his eyes, replayed that memory vividly in his mind, and pressed his thumb and middle finger together. He repeated this process several times, reinforcing the feeling. The next time he felt doubt creeping in during a trial, he used the anchor, and to his surprise, the surge of confidence from that first victory flooded back. From that moment, Alex became known not just for his skills but for his unshakeable poise.

Step-by-Step Guide: Creating Personal Emotional Anchors

1. **Identify the Desired Emotional State**:
   - Decide which emotional state you want to anchor, such as confidence, focus, or calmness. Reflect on a time when you felt this emotion intensely.
2. **Select a Physical Trigger**:
   - Choose a simple gesture, such as pressing your thumb and forefinger together, clenching your fist, or taking a deep breath. The action should be subtle enough to use in any situation, including during trials.
3. **Recall the Peak Emotional Experience**:
   - Close your eyes and vividly recall the moment when you felt the desired emotion most powerfully. Imagine every detail: what you saw, heard, felt, and even smelled. Immerse yourself fully in the experience.
4. **Activate the Physical Trigger at the Peak of the Emotion**:
   - As you relive the memory and feel the emotion building to its peak, activate your physical trigger (e.g., press your fingers together). Repeat this several times, each time fully immersing yourself in the memory while activating the trigger.
5. **Test the Anchor in Low-Pressure Situations**:
   - Before using the anchor in a high-stakes setting, test it in a low-pressure environment. Trigger the anchor and observe if the emotional state

returns. If it does, practice it consistently to strengthen the association.

Practical Application: Anchoring Techniques for Different Legal Scenarios

1. **Trial Lawyering**:
   o Create anchors for confidence and focus to use before or during opening statements and cross-examinations. For example, just before stepping into the courtroom, use the anchor to access a state of clarity and assertiveness.
2. **Calendar Negotiations with DAs**:
   o In negotiations, an anchor for calmness can be invaluable. Use a gesture such as placing a hand on your chest to activate calmness and maintain composure, ensuring that you communicate clearly and effectively.
3. **Motion Hearings**:
   o Before arguing a motion, activate your anchor for focus to sharpen your thoughts and presentation. This ensures that you stay on point and adapt quickly to the judge's questions or opposing counsel's arguments.

Triggering Anchors Under Pressure: Accessing Emotional States on Demand

The Moment of Activation: Using Anchors in High-Stress Situations

Once an anchor is established, the next step is learning how to trigger it effectively under pressure. The key to successfully activating an anchor is consistency and practice. By using the same gesture or action in similar situations, the emotional state becomes increasingly accessible, even in the most stressful moments.

Imagine you're moments away from delivering a closing argument, and you feel a surge of anxiety. You've practiced your confidence anchor—a subtle press of your thumb and forefinger—numerous times in preparation. As the pressure mounts, you take a deep breath, activate the anchor, and feel the familiar wave of confidence wash over you, enabling you to present your case assertively.

The Attorney Who Mastered Anchors Under Pressure

Rachel, a prosecutor, found herself feeling overwhelmed during a critical closing argument. Despite her preparation, the magnitude of the case made her second-guess herself. Remembering her anchor for confidence, which she had practiced using the gesture of clenching her fist, she took a deep breath and activated it. Almost instantly, she felt a rush of calm and certainty, recalling her previous successes. She delivered her closing argument with conviction, leading to a verdict in her favor. This experience reinforced for Rachel the power of properly built and practiced anchors.

Step-by-Step Guide: Effectively Triggering Anchors Under Pressure

1. **Take a Centering Breath Before Activating the Anchor**:
   o When you feel pressure building, take a deep breath to ground yourself. This helps you momentarily pause, creating space to access your anchor.
2. **Activate the Anchor Deliberately**:
   o Use the physical gesture you've practiced (e.g., pressing fingers together or placing a hand on your chest). Ensure it's done with intention and focus, fully committing to the gesture.
3. **Visualize the Peak Emotional State**:

o   As you activate the anchor, briefly visualize the memory associated with it. Imagine yourself in that powerful moment, feeling the confidence, calm, or focus returning to you.

4. **Practice Triggering the Anchor in Varying Situations**:
    o   Practice using your anchor in different environments, such as during mock trials, while preparing in your office, or even during routine negotiations. This builds muscle memory and strengthens the emotional response.

Practical Application: Triggering Anchors Across Legal Scenarios

1. **Jury Trials**:
    o   Use your confidence anchor just before delivering opening statements or conducting cross-examinations. The anchor can help you project authority and control, which jurors respond to positively.

2. **Juror Interactions**:
    o   When engaging with jurors during voir dire, activate a calmness anchor to maintain a relaxed demeanor. This helps build rapport, making jurors more receptive to your questions and presence.

3. **Motion Hearings and Pre-Trial Sessions**:
    o   Before entering the courtroom for a motion hearing, use a focus anchor to sharpen your mind. This ensures that your arguments are presented logically and convincingly, and that you can think on your feet when responding to the judge.

Anchoring Techniques for Self-Management in High-Stakes Legal Practice

Anchoring techniques for self-management provide attorneys with a powerful tool to control their emotional states, ensuring they remain confident, calm, and focused during high-pressure situations. By creating and consistently practicing personal anchors, attorneys can access these states on demand, transforming their approach to trial lawyering, negotiations, and other critical aspects of their practice. With mastery of these techniques, attorneys can turn their emotional responses into assets, strategically leveraging their state of mind to influence outcomes and deliver their best performance in every situation.

Anchoring Techniques with Witnesses: Building Trust and Confidence for Testimony

Witnesses play a critical role in the courtroom, and their demeanor and confidence can significantly impact how their testimony is perceived. Anchoring techniques with witnesses involve establishing and triggering positive emotional states, such as calmness, confidence, and clarity, to ensure that they perform well under pressure. By creating these anchors during witness preparation and using them strategically during testimony, attorneys can enhance witness credibility, build trust, and influence juror perception effectively.

Establishing Positive Anchors During Witness Preparation

The Foundation of Confidence: Creating Emotional Anchors for Witnesses

Establishing positive anchors for witnesses begins long before they take the stand. The objective is to associate a specific gesture or physical action with a positive emotional state—such as confidence, calmness, or clarity—so that the witness can access that state during testimony. This preparation helps witnesses manage nerves and recall important information without hesitation, increasing their effectiveness and credibility.

Imagine working with a nervous witness who struggles to maintain composure during questioning. To build an anchor for calmness, you guide the witness through a memory where they felt completely at ease, such as sitting on a beach or engaging in a favorite hobby. You then have them perform a subtle gesture, like placing their hand on their lap, while immersing themselves in that memory. By repeating this process several times, the witness learns to associate the gesture with the feeling of calm, creating a powerful anchor they can use during testimony.

The Attorney Who Prepared Her Witness with Anchoring

Emma, a defense attorney, faced a challenge when her key witness, Paul, showed signs of anxiety during their preparation sessions. Knowing that his calm demeanor was crucial for the case, she decided to establish a positive anchor. Emma asked Paul to recall a moment when he felt completely calm and confident—an experience from his childhood fishing on a quiet lake. She instructed him to close his eyes, visualize the scene, and place his hand gently on his knee. As Paul relived the memory, she guided him to repeat the gesture several times. By the end of their sessions, Paul could trigger this sense of calmness by simply placing his hand on his knee, a technique he used successfully during his testimony, leading to a favorable verdict.

Step-by-Step Guide: Establishing Positive Anchors in Witness Preparation

1. **Identify a Positive Emotional State**:

- o Ask the witness what state they would find most helpful during testimony—calmness, confidence, clarity, etc. Have them recall a specific memory where they felt this emotion intensely.
2. **Select a Simple, Subtle Gesture**:
   - o Choose a gesture that the witness can perform discreetly on the stand, such as placing a hand on their knee, tapping their thumb and finger together, or adjusting their glasses. The gesture should be easy to repeat without drawing attention.
3. **Guide the Witness Through the Memory**:
   - o Have the witness close their eyes and vividly recall the moment when they felt the desired emotion. Encourage them to visualize the sights, sounds, and sensations of the experience, immersing themselves fully.
4. **Associate the Gesture with the Emotional State**:
   - o As the witness reaches the peak of their emotional memory, instruct them to perform the chosen gesture. Repeat this process multiple times, each time reinforcing the association between the gesture and the emotional state.
5. **Practice in Simulated Testimonies**:
   - o Conduct mock testimony sessions where the witness practices using their anchor under questioning. This helps them become comfortable accessing the state in a trial-like setting, reinforcing their ability to use the anchor effectively.

Practical Application: Establishing Anchors for Witnesses Across Legal Scenarios

1. **Direct Examination Preparation**:
   - o During preparation, establish anchors for clarity and calmness so the witness can access these states easily while recounting details and responding to questions.

2. **Cross-Examination Defense**:
   o Prepare the witness to use their anchors when faced with aggressive cross-examination. This ensures they remain composed and focused, reducing the likelihood of contradictory or damaging statements.
3. **Pre-Trial Depositions**:
   o Establishing anchors during depositions provides the witness with tools to manage anxiety, ensuring their testimony remains consistent and credible even under pressure.

Triggering Familiar Positive States in Witnesses During Testimony

Guiding Witnesses to Access Positive States on the Stand

Once an anchor is established during preparation, it must be triggered effectively during testimony to be useful. Attorneys can subtly cue the witness to use their anchor when needed, or witnesses can independently activate their anchors when they feel anxiety or uncertainty. The goal is to create a seamless process where the witness feels empowered to manage their emotional state, maintaining credibility and consistency in their testimony.

For example, if a witness begins to show signs of nervousness, such as fidgeting or pausing, the attorney might ask a familiar, straightforward question designed to help the witness regain their composure. This question serves as a subtle reminder for the witness to use their anchor, helping them return to a calm and confident state.

The Prosecutor Who Triggered a Positive Anchor During Testimony

During a high-profile trial, prosecutor Jessica noticed her witness, Karen, becoming visibly anxious under cross-examination. Jessica had prepared Karen with an anchor for confidence—a slight tap of her thumb and index finger. To help Karen recall her anchor, Jessica asked, "Can you describe, in your own words, how you felt in that moment?" This familiar type of question, rehearsed during their preparation, acted as a cue for Karen to trigger her anchor. Karen tapped her fingers together, took a breath, and continued her testimony with renewed confidence. Her composed demeanor bolstered her credibility, contributing significantly to the prosecution's case.

Step-by-Step Guide: Triggering Anchors During Testimony

1. **Provide a Cue Through Familiar Questions**:
   o   If you notice the witness becoming nervous, ask a familiar question that mirrors those used during preparation sessions. This serves as a subtle reminder for the witness to use their anchor.
2. **Reinforce the Use of the Anchor Before Testimony**:
   o   Remind the witness to practice using their anchor just before entering the courtroom. A simple encouragement like, "Remember to use your anchor if you need it," helps reinforce the technique.
3. **Observe Body Language for Signs of Stress**:
   o   Watch for physical cues, such as fidgeting or avoidance of eye contact, that indicate the witness is becoming anxious. At this moment, a calming, familiar question can help prompt the use of their anchor.
4. **Follow Up with Supportive, Open-Ended Questions**:

- o To maintain the positive state, ask questions that allow the witness to speak freely about a topic they are confident in. This reinforces the emotional state associated with the anchor, making the witness more comfortable.

Practical Application: Triggering Anchors Across Legal Scenarios

1. **During Direct Examination**:
   - o Ensure that your line of questioning includes opportunities for the witness to use their anchor if needed. Ask open-ended, supportive questions that allow the witness to comfortably trigger their positive state.
2. **In High-Pressure Cross-Examination Situations**:
   - o When the opposing counsel's questions become intense, strategically interject with an objection or request for clarification, giving the witness a moment to activate their anchor discreetly.
3. **In Jury Trials**:
   - o Before testimony, remind the witness of their anchor and how to use it. During testimony, remain attentive, ready to ask a familiar, anchoring question if the witness shows signs of stress.

Practical Scripts: Employing Anchoring Techniques with Witnesses

1. **Establishing Anchors During Preparation**:
   - o "Think of a time when you felt completely calm and confident. Close your eyes and visualize every detail—where you were, what you saw, and how you felt. Now, as you feel that calm building, place your hand on your knee. Let's repeat this a few times."
2. **Triggering Anchors During Testimony**:

- o "Karen, tell us in your own words what you remember about the conversation that day." (This familiar phrasing, rehearsed during preparation, cues the witness to activate their anchor.)
3. **Encouraging Anchor Use Before Testimony**:
   - o "You've prepared well—remember to use your anchor if you feel nervous. It's there to help you stay focused and calm."

Anchoring Techniques for Building Effective Witness Testimony

Anchoring techniques with witnesses are essential for managing emotions and ensuring credibility during testimony. By establishing and practicing positive anchors during preparation, attorneys can equip witnesses with tools to access confidence, calmness, and clarity on demand. Triggering these anchors effectively during testimony allows witnesses to manage pressure, respond with composure, and maintain consistency in their accounts. Mastery of these techniques ensures that witnesses become assets in the courtroom, reinforcing the attorney's narrative and influencing juror perception positively.

Anchoring Juror Reactions: Guiding Perception and Engagement

In the courtroom, jurors are constantly interpreting information based not only on what they hear but also on what they see and feel. Anchoring techniques allow attorneys to subtly guide juror reactions by associating positive emotional states with key pieces of evidence or arguments. By using gestures, vocal patterns, and physical presence, attorneys can create positive anchors that enhance juror engagement and influence their perception. Equally important is avoiding negative anchors, which can create disengagement or skepticism. This section explores how to effectively employ these techniques to maximize impact and minimize negative reactions from jurors.

Using Gestures and Patterns: Associating Positive States with Key Evidence

The Art of Gestural Anchoring: Enhancing Engagement Through Physical Cues

Gestural anchoring involves using consistent gestures or patterns to link positive emotional states—such as trust, interest, or agreement—with key pieces of evidence or statements. When done effectively, these anchors reinforce positive reactions in jurors, making them more receptive to the attorney's message. By pairing gestures with specific pieces of evidence or arguments, attorneys can create subconscious associations that enhance the persuasiveness of their presentation.

For example, if an attorney presents a critical piece of evidence, they might use an open-palmed gesture, which signals transparency and trust. Over time, jurors begin to associate this gesture with important and reliable information. When the attorney repeats the gesture at later points in the trial, it reinforces the credibility of subsequent evidence, increasing jurors' receptiveness.

The Attorney Who Mastered Gestural Anchoring

David, a prosecutor, was known for his ability to keep jurors engaged and attentive. One of his key techniques involved gestural anchoring. During a trial where the defendant's DNA was a crucial piece of evidence, David used an open-palmed gesture each time he mentioned the DNA analysis, signaling openness and transparency. As the trial progressed, he continued to use the same gesture when discussing additional scientific evidence. Jurors became visibly more attentive, leaning forward and nodding as he spoke. The association between the gesture and the reliability of evidence became so strong that when David used it during closing arguments, the jury appeared fully engaged, ultimately delivering a guilty verdict.

Step-by-Step Guide: Creating Positive Gestural Anchors for Jurors

1. **Select a Positive Gesture**:
   - Choose a gesture that conveys trust, openness, or clarity. Common gestures include an open palm, a light nod, or a subtle forward lean. The gesture should be natural and easy to repeat throughout the trial.
2. **Associate the Gesture with Key Evidence or Arguments**:
   - Pair the gesture with critical pieces of evidence, such as forensic analysis or eyewitness testimony. Consistency is key; the more frequently the gesture is used in conjunction with reliable information, the stronger the association becomes.
3. **Reinforce the Gesture at Key Moments**:
   - Use the gesture when presenting new evidence that supports your case. This consistency builds a pattern that jurors begin to recognize, enhancing their perception of the evidence's credibility.
4. **Practice and Maintain Subtlety**:
   - Ensure that the gesture appears natural and integrated into your presentation style. Overly dramatic or exaggerated gestures can appear manipulative, which may lead to juror distrust.

Practical Application: Gestural Anchoring Across Legal Scenarios

1. **Opening Statements**:

- o Use an open-palmed gesture when outlining key points of the case. This establishes an initial sense of trust, making jurors more receptive to the evidence presented later.

2. **Cross-Examination**:
   - o If you want jurors to question the credibility of an opposing witness, use a different gesture, such as a slow nod or a slight tilt of the head, when highlighting discrepancies in their testimony. This subtly cues jurors to scrutinize the information more closely.

3. **Closing Arguments**:
   - o Reinforce the positive gesture established during the presentation of evidence. This consistency triggers the same positive state, helping jurors recall the credibility of your earlier arguments.

Avoiding Negative Anchors: Maintaining Juror Engagement and Trust

Navigating Potential Pitfalls: Identifying and Avoiding Negative Anchors

Negative anchors are gestures, phrases, or vocal patterns that inadvertently create disengagement, skepticism, or discomfort among jurors. These can occur when an attorney uses overly aggressive body language, raises their voice excessively, or repeatedly performs a gesture associated with uncertainty. Recognizing and avoiding these behaviors is crucial to maintaining juror trust and ensuring that their focus remains on the presented evidence rather than on their negative reaction to the delivery.

For instance, if an attorney frequently crosses their arms when presenting evidence, jurors may subconsciously perceive this as defensive or closed-off behavior, associating it with the information's unreliability. Being mindful of body language and verbal patterns is key to avoiding these unintended negative associations.

The Attorney Who Corrected a Negative Anchor

Sarah, a defense attorney, struggled during a trial where jurors appeared disengaged whenever she presented evidence. After reviewing footage of her own presentations, she noticed that she often crossed her arms and narrowed her eyes when discussing critical points. This defensive posture, she realized, could be creating a negative anchor, signaling to jurors that she herself was not confident in the evidence. In response, she consciously shifted to using an open-palmed gesture, maintaining an upright posture and a warm expression. The change was immediate; jurors seemed more attentive and responsive, and Sarah's client ultimately received a favorable verdict.

Step-by-Step Guide: Avoiding Negative Anchors and Maintaining Positive Juror Engagement

1. **Identify Potential Negative Gestures or Patterns**:
   o Review your presentations and identify any gestures that may come across as defensive (e.g., crossing arms), aggressive (e.g., pointing fingers), or closed off (e.g., turning away from the jury).
2. **Replace Negative Gestures with Neutral or Positive Alternatives**:
   o If you notice negative patterns, consciously replace them with gestures that convey openness, such as open hands, light nods, or leaning slightly forward to show engagement.
3. **Monitor Juror Reactions**:
   o Pay attention to jurors' body language. If they appear disengaged—such as crossing their arms or leaning back—evaluate your delivery for potential negative anchors. Adjust accordingly to re-establish a positive connection.
4. **Practice Maintaining Neutrality During High-Pressure Moments**:
   o During intense cross-examinations or objections, maintain an open posture and avoid defensive

gestures. This consistency helps jurors view you as confident and in control, even when the trial becomes contentious.

Practical Application: Avoiding Negative Anchors Across Legal Scenarios

1. **Motion Hearings**:
   o When arguing motions before a judge, avoid defensive gestures such as crossing arms or pointing. Instead, use a balanced, open stance to convey confidence and reliability.
2. **Interactions with Opposing Counsel**:
   o During calendar negotiations or sidebar discussions, remain aware of your gestures. Avoid aggressive patterns that may create an adversarial atmosphere, opting instead for gestures that convey cooperation and professionalism.
3. **Jury Trials**:
   o Throughout the trial, especially during opening statements and closing arguments, consciously choose gestures that maintain openness and engagement, avoiding any postures or patterns that might create a negative association.

Practical Scripts: Employing and Avoiding Anchors with Jurors

1. **Positive Anchoring During Evidence Presentation**:
   o "As you can see from this evidence..." (Open palm gesture) "...this clearly supports the timeline of events."
   o The open palm reinforces transparency and builds trust.
2. **Avoiding Negative Anchors During Cross-Examination**:

- Avoid crossing arms or leaning away when questioning a witness. Instead, keep hands open or gently resting on the podium, maintaining an engaged and attentive posture.
3. **Positive Reinforcement in Closing Arguments**:
   - "You've seen the evidence, and you understand the truth..." (Consistent open-palmed gesture used throughout the trial) "...now it's time for justice."
   - The repetition of a trusted gesture reinforces credibility and ensures a cohesive, positive state among jurors.

Mastering Juror Anchoring Techniques for Persuasive Communication

Anchoring juror reactions is a nuanced and powerful skill that requires careful attention to physical cues, gestures, and patterns. By effectively using positive anchors, attorneys can create associations that enhance juror engagement, trust, and receptiveness. Avoiding negative anchors ensures that jurors remain focused and open, free from subconscious signals that may disengage or bias them. Mastering these techniques allows attorneys to strategically guide jurors' emotional and cognitive responses, creating an environment where the evidence presented is perceived as credible, persuasive, and aligned with the attorney's narrative.

Anchoring the Dishonest, Hostile Witness During Cross-Examination: Turning the Tables

Cross-examining a dishonest or hostile witness is a high-stakes endeavor where an attorney's ability to control the emotional and behavioral dynamics can make or break the case. Anchoring techniques provide powerful strategies for attorneys to manage and influence the state of such witnesses, exposing dishonesty or reducing hostility in a way that becomes evident to the jury. By establishing anchors that elicit discomfort or uncertainty in a hostile witness, attorneys can gain control of the cross-examination, leading the witness to reveal inconsistencies or weaken their credibility. This section delves into the art of anchoring in these challenging scenarios, offering practical guidance for employing these techniques effectively.

Understanding the Hostile Witness: Setting the Stage for Anchoring

Hostile Witnesses: Identifying the Tactics and Behaviors

A hostile witness is one who is either uncooperative, dishonest, or overly defensive during questioning. Such witnesses may deliberately evade questions, provide misleading information, or attempt to disrupt the flow of cross-examination. Recognizing these behaviors early on is crucial, as it allows the attorney to develop a strategy that utilizes anchoring techniques to create discomfort, highlight dishonesty, or subtly shift the witness's emotional state.

Imagine an expert witness brought in by the opposing side who begins to evade questions or provides ambiguous answers designed to confuse the jury. By carefully observing their body language and verbal patterns, an attorney can identify when the witness is becoming defensive or dishonest, setting the stage for anchoring techniques that exploit these moments to undermine the witness's credibility.

The Attorney Who Anchored a Hostile Witness

During a high-profile fraud trial, defense attorney James faced a hostile witness—an accountant who had been paid by the prosecution to testify against his client. The witness dodged questions, provided vague answers, and seemed intent on frustrating the defense's line of inquiry. James, however, was prepared. He noticed that each time the witness lied, they averted their eyes and fidgeted with their pen. Recognizing this behavior, James began subtly mirroring the witness's actions during key questions, making the witness visibly uncomfortable. As the cross-examination progressed, James anchored these gestures to specific moments, creating an association that made the witness appear increasingly defensive and dishonest to the jury. The jury eventually found the witness's testimony unreliable, and James's client was acquitted.

Establishing Anchors: Creating Discomfort in Dishonest Witnesses

The Setup: Using Subtle Cues to Anchor Dishonest Behavior

Anchoring a dishonest witness begins with observing their natural responses when they provide dishonest or evasive answers. These could be physical behaviors such as avoiding eye contact, crossing arms, fidgeting, or shifting posture. Once these patterns are identified, the attorney can anchor these cues by mirroring them or subtly incorporating a repeated gesture or phrase when the witness exhibits the behavior. Over time, the witness becomes conditioned to associate discomfort with their own dishonesty, making it more challenging for them to lie convincingly.

Step-by-Step Guide: Establishing Anchors for Dishonesty

1. **Observe and Identify Behavioral Patterns**:
    o   Watch for specific physical responses when the witness lies or evades—such as looking away, touching their face, or shifting in their chair.
2. **Introduce a Subtle Anchor**:

- o Choose a gesture that you can repeat each time the witness exhibits the dishonest behavior, such as a slight nod, a specific tone, or adjusting your glasses. The key is consistency—use the gesture every time the witness behaves dishonestly.
3. **Build the Association**:
   - o As the anchor is used consistently with dishonest behavior, the witness becomes conditioned to feel discomfort when the gesture is repeated. This discomfort becomes visible to the jury, making the witness appear less credible.
4. **Escalate the Technique Strategically**:
   - o As the witness becomes increasingly uncomfortable, begin asking more direct questions that highlight inconsistencies. The combination of discomfort and direct questioning can cause the witness to falter, revealing the truth or further exposing their dishonesty.

Practical Application: Anchoring Dishonest Witnesses Across Legal Scenarios

1. **Cross-Examination in High-Stakes Trials**:
   - o Use anchoring to create a visible pattern of discomfort when the witness evades or lies. For example, if the witness avoids eye contact during certain questions, nod subtly each time, reinforcing the association between their dishonesty and discomfort.
2. **Motion Hearings**:
   - o In hearings where expert witnesses may be biased, apply anchoring techniques to expose their inconsistencies. If an expert shows discomfort when pressed on technical details, reinforce the pattern with a repeated gesture, such as pausing briefly before questioning again.
3. **Depositions and Pre-Trial Interviews**:

- o Establish anchors early by observing the witness's reactions in depositions. This allows you to refine the technique, ensuring that the same anchor will trigger discomfort during trial testimony.

Triggering Anchors During Cross-Examination: Amplifying the Witness's Discomfort

Guiding the Witness to a Breaking Point: Using Anchors Strategically

Once an anchor has been established, the next step is triggering it at key moments during cross-examination. The goal is to amplify the witness's discomfort when they lie or evade, making it evident to the jury that the witness is not being truthful. This can be done through strategic questioning and timing, where the attorney subtly repeats the anchor (e.g., a gesture or phrase) as they press for details.

For instance, if the witness has been anchored to discomfort when they shift in their chair, the attorney might lean slightly forward and repeat a key phrase like, "Just to clarify..." each time the witness displays this behavior. This repetition creates a visible pattern, making the witness's discomfort more obvious to the jury and signaling that the witness is being evasive.

The Prosecutor Who Triggered Anchors to Unravel a Witness

Lisa, a prosecutor, was cross-examining a hostile witness who had provided false testimony to protect the defendant. Lisa had noticed during the deposition that whenever the witness lied, they would scratch their chin. During the trial, Lisa used this behavior as an anchor. Each time the witness scratched their chin, Lisa leaned slightly forward and asked, "Let's revisit that statement." The witness, visibly uncomfortable, began to stammer, scratching their chin more frequently. As the jury observed this pattern, the witness's credibility deteriorated, and the prosecution's case was strengthened.

Step-by-Step Guide: Triggering Anchors Effectively

1. **Prepare the Triggering Strategy**:
   - Before the trial, review the witness's behavior from depositions and pre-trial sessions. Plan which anchors to use and how to trigger them during key questions.
2. **Use Strategic Questions**:
   - Begin with open-ended questions that allow the witness to answer freely. When they display dishonest behavior, use the anchor consistently—such as repeating a specific phrase ("Just to clarify...") or gesture (leaning forward).
3. **Increase the Intensity Gradually**:
   - As the witness becomes more visibly uncomfortable, ask more pointed and direct questions that focus on inconsistencies. This escalation, combined with the repeated anchor, increases the witness's discomfort, leading them to reveal dishonesty or falter under pressure.
4. **Maintain Control and Professionalism**:
   - Ensure that your gestures and tone remain subtle and professional. The goal is to appear calm and composed, reinforcing the perception that the witness is the one struggling to maintain credibility.

Practical Application: Triggering Anchors During Legal Proceedings

1. **Cross-Examination**:

o During cross-examination, use gestures or phrases that reinforce the discomfort associated with dishonesty. For example, lean forward each time the witness shows signs of evasion, signaling that they are becoming increasingly defensive.

2. **Jury Trials**:
   o Jurors are perceptive and will notice patterns. By repeating the anchor at moments when the witness is evasive, you create a visual and auditory pattern that jurors can connect to dishonesty, enhancing the persuasive impact of your cross-examination.

3. **Motion Hearings**:
   o When questioning witnesses who may be biased, apply anchors to create a pattern of discomfort. This demonstrates to the judge that the witness may not be reliable, strengthening your argument.

Practical Scripts: Employing Anchoring Techniques with Dishonest, Hostile Witnesses

1. **Establishing the Anchor During Cross-Examination**:
   o "Now, you mentioned earlier that you were certain about the time. Could you clarify exactly what time you arrived?" (Watch for evasive behavior and introduce the anchor—a light nod each time.)

2. **Triggering the Anchor for Maximum Effect**:
   o "Let's go back to your earlier statement. You said you didn't see anything unusual, correct?" (If the witness shifts or fidgets, lean slightly forward and repeat the same question.)

3. **Reinforcing the Pattern During Closing Arguments**:
   o "You saw how the witness reacted every time they were asked to clarify. Their discomfort spoke louder than words—revealing the truth behind their evasions."

Mastering Anchoring Techniques for Hostile Witnesses

Anchoring techniques for managing dishonest and hostile witnesses offer attorneys powerful tools to expose deception and maintain control during cross-examination. By observing and establishing patterns of discomfort, attorneys can create associations that reveal the witness's dishonesty to the jury. Triggering these anchors effectively requires precision, patience, and subtlety, ensuring that the witness's credibility diminishes while the attorney's control and professionalism remain evident. Mastering these techniques equips attorneys with the strategic advantage needed to turn even the most challenging witnesses into assets for their case.

Example: Employing Anchoring Techniques During Direct and Cross-Examination

In this example, we'll explore how an attorney (defense attorney Michael) would observe the (witness John) while the district attorney (DA) conducts the direct examination. During direct-examination, Michael would watch for signs of dishonesty or discomfort and take note of patterns or behaviors (e.g., avoiding eye contact, fidgeting) that he can later use during his own cross-examination. The goal is to demonstrate how these techniques can be applied to manage emotions, build credibility, and highlight inconsistencies effectively. The witness, John, is a key player in the case—he claims to have seen the defendant near the crime scene at the time of the incident. However, the defense suspects that John's testimony is biased and influenced by external factors, such as pressure from the prosecution.

Observation During Direct Examination

During the DA's direct examination, Michael closely observes John, the witness, for any signs of discomfort or dishonesty. He notes that when the DA asks John specific questions about the time and details of the incident, John becomes visibly uncomfortable—he shifts in his seat and touches his face frequently. Michael makes a mental note of these behaviors, understanding that they indicate discomfort when John is trying to recall (or fabricate) details.

Michael's objective is to use these observed behaviors as cues during his cross-examination to anchor John's discomfort when he reveals inconsistencies or lies. This strategy will make it easier for Michael to expose John's unreliability to the jury.

Cross-Examination: Applying Anchoring Techniques

Now that Michael has noted John's discomfort cues (shifting in his seat and touching his face), he plans his approach for cross-examination. He will use these cues to establish and reinforce anchors, making John's dishonesty more apparent to the jury.

Cross-Examination: Setting Up the Discomfort Anchor

Michael: "John, you testified earlier that you saw the defendant near the alley. Let's go over those details again— can you tell me exactly what time this was?"

(Michael observes John's body language as he asks the question. As expected, John shifts in his seat and touches his face—behaviors indicating discomfort. Michael leans forward slightly and repeats the question.)

John: "I believe it was around 3 PM."

(Michael tilts his head—a subtle gesture he plans to repeat whenever John shows signs of discomfort—reinforcing the association between John's evasive behavior and discomfort.)

Michael: "Just to clarify, you said earlier it was around 2 PM. Is it 2 or 3?"

(John fidgets again, touching his face.)

Michael: "You seem unsure, John. Could it be possible that you didn't see the defendant clearly at that time?"

(Michael tilts his head again as John displays discomfort.)

John: "Well, I... I think it was around 2, but I'm not completely certain."

By repeating his head tilt and leaning in whenever John shows these discomfort behaviors, Michael creates a pattern that links John's evasive behavior with visible discomfort. This pattern becomes a visual cue for the jury, signaling that John may be unsure or dishonest when responding to specific questions.

Escalating the Cross-Examination: Reinforcing the Discomfort Anchor

As the cross-examination continues, Michael escalates his questioning to emphasize inconsistencies while using his anchoring techniques.

Michael: "Let's go back to your initial statement to the police, John. Did you mention the exact time when you saw the person who looked like the defendant?"

(John scratches his chin—a behavior Michael noted during the DA's direct examination as a discomfort cue.)

(Michael leans forward slightly, repeating his anchoring gesture.)

John: "I... I don't remember exactly."

Michael: "Is it fair to say that you're not completely sure you saw my client at that time?"

(Michael tilts his head once more as John shifts in his seat.)

John: "Yes, it's possible."

At this point, Michael has consistently used the tilt and forward lean as anchors each time John exhibits discomfort. The jury sees the pattern: John becomes visibly uneasy when he is unsure or inconsistent, reinforcing Michael's narrative that John's testimony is unreliable.

Practical Conclusion of Cross-Examination

By the end of the cross-examination, Michael has effectively used the discomfort anchor to highlight the witness's inconsistencies. The jury, having seen the pattern of discomfort whenever John's statements are challenged, perceives John's testimony as unreliable.

Summary of Techniques Used

1. **Observation During Direct Examination**:
   o Michael pays close attention to John's behaviors when the DA asks specific questions, noting discomfort cues such as shifting in his seat or touching his face. These observations are crucial for planning his cross-examination strategy.
2. **Cross-Examination Techniques**:
   o **Discomfort Anchoring**: Michael uses subtle gestures like tilting his head or leaning forward whenever John shows signs of discomfort. This reinforces the pattern that links John's discomfort with his evasiveness or dishonesty.
   o **Strategic Questioning**: Michael escalates the questioning by focusing on inconsistencies and repeating the anchor whenever John reacts with

discomfort, ensuring the jury recognizes the
pattern.

3. **Jury Perception**:

   o By establishing and reinforcing the discomfort
     anchor, Michael makes John's discomfort visible
     and creates a clear link between his evasiveness
     and dishonesty. This strategy makes it easier for
     the jury to doubt John's credibility.

Mastering Anchoring Techniques for Hostile Witnesses

By first observing the witness during direct examination and
then strategically applying discomfort anchors during cross-
examination, attorneys can effectively manage witness
behavior, expose inconsistencies, and guide jury perception.
This approach ensures that hostile or dishonest witnesses
are framed in a way that undermines their credibility,
aligning with the defense's strategy and narrative.

As we move into the realm of advanced non-verbal
techniques, we delve deeper into the subtleties of body
language and sensory feedback that can provide attorneys
with powerful insights and influence in the courtroom. These
advanced techniques build on foundational NLP skills,
allowing attorneys to read and interpret eye movements for
deeper understanding, observe micro-expressions and subtle
body shifts to gauge emotional states, and employ strategic
interventions to disrupt uncooperative patterns during
witness testimony. This section covers eye accessing cues,
calibration methods for heightened sensory acuity, and the
use of pattern interrupts—essential tools for maintaining
control and effectively managing witness behavior, juror
engagement, and courtroom dynamics.

5. Mastering the Subtleties: Advanced Non-Verbal Techniques for Insight and Influence

In the courtroom, subtle shifts in eye movements, facial expressions, and body language can reveal far more than words alone. Advanced non-verbal techniques allow attorneys to decode these cues, providing crucial insights into the thoughts and emotions of witnesses and jurors. This section explores the art of reading eye accessing cues, using calibration and sensory acuity to observe micro-expressions and body language shifts, and applying pattern interrupts to regain control when witness testimony becomes uncooperative. By mastering these techniques, attorneys can gain a strategic advantage, adapting their responses and maintaining control over courtroom dynamics with precision and finesse.

Reading Eye Accessing Cues: Gaining Insight Through Eye Movements

Eye accessing cues are a powerful tool in the realm of non-verbal communication, allowing attorneys to gain insight into the internal thought processes of witnesses, jurors, and even opposing counsel. The idea behind eye accessing cues, rooted in NLP, is that the direction in which people move their eyes when processing information reveals whether they are recalling a memory, constructing an image, or accessing their emotions. By understanding these cues, attorneys can gauge the credibility of witnesses, assess juror reactions, and adapt their strategies in real time. This section provides a comprehensive guide to mastering this technique, offering practical applications and strategies for trial lawyering.

Understanding Eye Accessing Cues: The Window to Internal Processing

The Basics of Eye Movement: Interpreting Direction and Meaning

In NLP, eye accessing cues suggest that when a person looks in a specific direction, they are accessing a particular mode of thought or sensory information. The standard model identifies the following cues:

- **Upward and to the Right (Visually Constructed Images)**: This movement indicates the person is imagining or constructing an image. It might suggest that they are creating a visual scenario that hasn't occurred, which can be useful for identifying deception.
- **Upward and to the Left (Visually Remembered Images)**: When someone looks in this direction, they are likely recalling a real visual memory. This can help verify whether a witness is remembering an actual event.
- **Lateral Right (Auditory Constructed)**: Looking to the right laterally suggests that the person is fabricating sounds or words, useful when determining if someone is making up a story.
- **Lateral Left (Auditory Remembered)**: This indicates that the person is recalling sounds they've heard before, which may validate a witness's recounting of a conversation.
- **Downward and to the Right (Kinesthetic Feelings)**: A downward glance to the right indicates that the person is accessing their feelings or bodily sensations. This can reveal emotional reactions or stress levels.
- **Downward and to the Left (Internal Dialogue)**: When someone looks downward to the left, they are often engaging in internal dialogue. This can signal that they are processing or evaluating their own thoughts or emotions.

By observing these cues, attorneys can interpret whether a person is recalling genuine memories, constructing false narratives, or processing emotions. This knowledge provides valuable leverage in various legal contexts, from assessing a witness's credibility to gauging juror reactions.

The Attorney Who Decoded Eye Movements

Consider Sarah, a seasoned trial lawyer, who faced a critical witness whose testimony was central to the prosecution's case. During direct examination, the witness claimed to have clearly seen the defendant at the crime scene. Sarah, observing the witness's eye movements, noticed that when asked to describe what they saw, the witness's eyes moved upward and to the right—a classic cue for visually constructed images. Suspecting that the witness was fabricating the story, Sarah adjusted her cross-examination approach, asking the witness for further details and tracking their eye movements. Each time the witness described the scene, their eyes consistently moved upward and to the right. Sarah's use of eye accessing cues allowed her to expose the inconsistency to the jury, ultimately weakening the prosecution's case.

Step-by-Step Guide: Using Eye Accessing Cues in Legal Practice

1. **Familiarize Yourself with Eye Accessing Cues**:
   - Study the standard eye accessing cues in NLP to understand what each movement typically indicates (e.g., visually remembered vs. constructed images).
2. **Observe Baseline Behavior**:
   - Before interpreting eye movements, observe the person's baseline behavior during neutral questioning or when they are relaxed. This helps you differentiate between their natural eye movements and those triggered by specific questions.

3. **Ask Calibrating Questions**:
   - Ask questions that you already know the answer to, such as "What color is your car?" or "What did you have for breakfast?" Observe the person's eye movements as they access these genuine memories. This establishes a baseline for how they recall real information.
4. **Ask Targeted Questions and Observe Reactions**:
   - Once you have the baseline, move on to more targeted questions related to the case. Observe if the eye movements match the expected pattern for truthful responses (e.g., visually remembered) or if they shift to cues indicating constructed or fabricated information (e.g., visually constructed).
5. **Correlate Eye Movements with Other Non-Verbal Cues**:
   - Combine eye accessing cues with other signs such as micro-expressions, body language, or changes in voice pitch to build a comprehensive picture of the person's state of mind.
6. **Practice Interpretation Across Different Scenarios**:
   - Use mock trials or practice sessions with colleagues to refine your skills in interpreting eye cues. This helps you become confident in recognizing patterns and reacting to them in real time during actual court proceedings.

Practical Application: Using Eye Accessing Cues Across Legal Scenarios

1. **Witness Cross-Examination**:
   - Track eye movements as the witness responds to your questions. If they frequently look up and to the right when asked to describe the crime scene, this could indicate they are constructing details rather than recalling genuine memories. Use this as a basis for further questioning to challenge their credibility.

2. **Juror Interactions During Voir Dire**:
   o During jury selection, ask potential jurors about their attitudes toward certain legal concepts (e.g., self-defense, circumstantial evidence) and observe their eye movements. This can provide insights into whether they are recalling genuine thoughts or constructing responses they believe you want to hear.
3. **Negotiations with Opposing Counsel**:
   o In negotiations, when discussing settlement terms, observe eye movements to gauge whether opposing counsel is genuinely recalling past case precedents or fabricating a scenario to gain leverage. This can inform your strategy and response.
4. **Calendar Hearings and Motion Hearings**:
   o Track the judge's eye movements when presenting evidence or making arguments. While this requires a subtle approach, understanding how the judge processes information (e.g., looking up to visually recall case facts) can help tailor your presentation for maximum impact.

Practical Scripts: Applying Eye Accessing Cues During Examination

1. **Establishing the Baseline with a Witness**:
   o "John, before we get into the details of that day, let me ask—what color is your car?" *(Observe the eye movement when the witness recalls a genuine memory.)*
   o "Now, can you describe what you had for breakfast yesterday?" *(Confirm the same eye movement as before to establish the baseline.)*
2. **Targeting Inconsistencies During Cross-Examination**:
   o "You mentioned that you saw the defendant at the scene. Can you describe exactly what he was wearing?" *(If the witness looks up and to the*

117

right, follow up with additional detailed questions to probe further and expose inconsistency.)

3. **Assessing Jurors During Voir Dire**:
   o "Do you believe that people who are charged with crimes are generally guilty, or do you feel everyone deserves a fair chance?" *(Observe eye movements to determine if they are recalling a genuine opinion or constructing a socially acceptable response.)*

Advanced Strategies: Combining Eye Accessing Cues with Other Techniques

Sensory Acuity: Enhancing the Interpretation of Eye Movements

To maximize the effectiveness of eye accessing cues, attorneys should combine them with sensory acuity techniques—observing other subtle shifts like facial expressions, tone of voice, and posture. For example, if a witness's eyes move laterally right (indicating auditory construction) and their voice pitch rises slightly, it may suggest that they are fabricating details of a conversation. By combining cues, the attorney gains a more accurate understanding of the witness's credibility.

Pattern Interrupts: Redirecting the Eye Movement

When an attorney notices a witness frequently looking in a direction that indicates fabrication, they can use pattern interrupts—subtle shifts in tone or pacing of questions—to disrupt the witness's focus. This momentarily unsettles the witness, making it easier for the attorney to challenge inconsistencies or get more truthful responses.

Example Scenario: Using Eye Accessing Cues During Cross-Examination

Case Context: The defense attorney, Alex, is cross-examining a key witness for the prosecution, Samantha, who claims to have seen the defendant at the scene of a robbery. Alex suspects that Samantha's testimony may have been influenced or fabricated. During the prosecution's direct examination, Alex observed Samantha's eye movements when she was asked specific questions. Alex noticed that when Samantha was recalling details about the robbery, she frequently looked upward and to the right—a classic indicator in NLP of someone constructing visual images rather than recalling a genuine memory. Armed with this observation, Alex prepares to use this insight during cross-examination.

Cross-Examination: Applying Eye Accessing Cues

Establishing the Baseline

Before diving into the critical details of the robbery, Alex first establishes a baseline for Samantha's eye movements when she is recalling genuine memories.

Alex: "Samantha, before we discuss the events of that day, I'd like to ask a few quick questions to understand your background. Can you tell me what color your car is?"

(Samantha looks upward and to the left, indicating she is visually recalling a memory. Alex notes this movement as a genuine memory cue.)

Samantha: "It's blue."

Alex: "And what did you have for breakfast this morning?"

(Again, Samantha looks upward and to the left, confirming Alex's baseline observation that she looks in this direction when recalling genuine memories.)

Samantha: "I had eggs and toast."

(Alex is now confident that Samantha's natural eye movement when recalling genuine visual information is upward and to the left.)

Moving to the Critical Details

Now that Alex has established a baseline, he shifts to questioning Samantha about the robbery, carefully observing her eye movements for any signs of inconsistency.

Alex: "Samantha, you mentioned earlier that you saw the defendant at the scene. Can you describe exactly where you were standing when you saw him?"

(Samantha looks upward and to the right—a departure from her baseline direction for recalling genuine memories. Alex notes this as a cue that she may be constructing the memory.)

Samantha: "I was standing across the street, near the entrance to the coffee shop."

(Alex notices the shift in eye movement and decides to press further.)

Alex: "And you saw him clearly? What was he wearing?"

(Samantha again looks upward and to the right, indicating a constructed visual image.)

Samantha: "He was wearing a black hoodie and jeans."

Testing the Consistency of the Eye Movements

Alex now has enough evidence to suspect that Samantha is constructing her answers rather than recalling genuine memories. He decides to test her further by comparing her eye movements against other, less critical information.

Alex: "Interesting. Earlier, you mentioned that you were at the coffee shop. Can you tell me the name of the shop again?"

(Samantha looks upward and to the left, indicating she is genuinely recalling the name.)

Samantha: "It's called 'Brew & Beans.'"

(Alex's observation confirms that when Samantha recalls genuine information, her eyes move upward and to the left, as established in the baseline. The fact that her eyes move upward and to the right when describing the defendant suggests fabrication.)

Challenging the Witness Using the Eye Accessing Cues

Now that Alex has a clear pattern, he uses his findings to challenge Samantha's credibility directly.

Alex: "Samantha, I noticed that when I asked you about your car and breakfast earlier, you looked in one direction. But when I asked about the defendant's appearance, you looked in a completely different direction. Can you explain why that is?"

(Samantha appears taken aback, and her eyes dart downward, a cue that she's engaging in internal dialogue and likely feeling uncomfortable.)

Samantha: "I... I'm not sure. I guess I was just trying to remember."

Alex: "You see, people's eyes naturally move in a particular direction when they're recalling genuine memories. But when they construct images or fabricate details, their eyes tend to move differently. It seems like your eyes move differently when talking about the defendant. Are you sure you saw him as clearly as you say?"

(Samantha's discomfort increases, and she begins to shift in her seat—another cue of unease. She looks downward and to the right, accessing her feelings and likely feeling pressure.)

Samantha: "I... I mean, I think so, but it was all happening so fast."

Wrapping Up the Cross-Examination

Alex's questioning and his observations of Samantha's eye accessing cues have effectively created doubt in the jury's mind about the credibility of her testimony. By linking her eye movements to her credibility and showing the jury that she may have been fabricating details, Alex has undermined the prosecution's witness without directly accusing her of lying—allowing the jury to draw their own conclusions.

Summary of Techniques Used

1. **Establishing the Baseline**:
   o Alex asks simple questions (e.g., about Samantha's car and breakfast) to observe her eye movements when recalling genuine memories. This helps Alex determine her natural baseline.
2. **Observing the Deviation**:
   o Alex shifts to asking about the robbery and notices that Samantha's eye movements deviate from her baseline. When she describes seeing

the defendant, her eyes move upward and to the right, suggesting she is constructing the image rather than recalling a genuine memory.

3. **Testing Consistency**:
   o Alex intersperses unrelated questions (e.g., about the coffee shop name) to confirm the baseline pattern. This allows him to differentiate between genuine recall and constructed responses.

4. **Challenging the Witness**:
   o Alex uses his observations to confront Samantha, creating discomfort and further inconsistency in her responses. He references her eye movements to subtly indicate to the jury that she may not be telling the truth, planting seeds of doubt.

In this example, Alex effectively uses eye accessing cues to detect inconsistencies and strategically challenge the witness's testimony. By establishing a baseline and comparing it against the witness's behavior during critical questions, Alex creates a clear pattern that the jury can understand, reinforcing his argument without overtly accusing the witness of dishonesty. This approach demonstrates the powerful role that eye accessing cues can play in courtroom strategy, allowing attorneys to gain insights into the credibility of witnesses and adapt their techniques for maximum impact.

Mastering Eye Accessing Cues for Legal Advantage

Reading eye accessing cues is a nuanced skill that provides attorneys with invaluable insights into the thoughts and emotions of witnesses, jurors, and opposing counsel. By understanding and interpreting these subtle movements, attorneys can strategically adapt their questioning techniques, assess credibility, and influence courtroom dynamics. Mastery of eye accessing cues, combined with other non-verbal and sensory acuity skills, ensures that attorneys remain one step ahead, turning subtle visual signals into powerful tools for legal persuasion and strategy.

Calibration and Sensory Acuity: The Art of Perceiving the Subtle

Calibration and sensory acuity are essential skills for mastering non-verbal communication in the courtroom. These techniques involve observing and interpreting micro-expressions, subtle shifts in body language, and other nuanced physical cues to gauge the emotional and mental states of witnesses, jurors, or even opposing counsel. By fine-tuning these observational skills, attorneys can adapt their strategies and responses in real-time, ensuring they maintain control and maximize their persuasive impact. This section provides a comprehensive guide to honing these skills, offering practical applications, stories, and techniques tailored for trial lawyering.

What is Calibration? Understanding the Subtle Dance of Interaction

The Basics: Defining Calibration and Sensory Acuity

Calibration in NLP refers to the process of establishing a baseline for an individual's natural, non-verbal behaviors and then observing deviations from that baseline to interpret their emotional and cognitive states. Sensory acuity enhances this process by sharpening one's ability to detect the smallest shifts in behavior, such as micro-expressions, changes in posture, or variations in breathing.

These skills are essential for attorneys, as they allow for real-time analysis of how a witness is feeling, whether a juror is engaged or skeptical, or if opposing counsel is confident or uncertain. By calibrating effectively, attorneys can respond dynamically, adapting their questioning or arguments to maintain influence and control over the courtroom.

Micro-Expressions: The Hidden Language of Emotion

Micro-Expressions: Brief, Unfiltered Windows into Emotion

Micro-expressions are fleeting facial expressions that occur when someone tries to conceal their true emotions. These expressions typically last only a fraction of a second but can reveal significant insights into a person's emotional state. In the context of a trial, observing micro-expressions can help an attorney determine if a witness is feeling fear, anger, or confusion, even if they are trying to maintain a composed exterior.

The Attorney Who Caught the Unfiltered Expression

During a high-stakes trial, defense attorney Rachel noticed a quick flash of discomfort on the face of a prosecution witness when asked about their relationship with the defendant. The witness had maintained a calm demeanor up until that point, but Rachel caught the micro-expression—an involuntary tightening of the lips and a slight furrow of the brow—indicating discomfort and possibly dishonesty. Sensing an opportunity, Rachel adjusted her questioning, probing deeper into the relationship. The witness's testimony unraveled, exposing inconsistencies that helped sway the jury in her client's favor.

Step-by-Step Guide: Observing Micro-Expressions

1. **Calibrate the Baseline**:
    - Observe the individual during neutral questioning or casual conversation to establish

their typical expressions and behaviors when they are comfortable.

2. **Ask Calibrating Questions**:
   - Use simple, non-threatening questions like "How long have you been working at your current job?" to observe their baseline responses.

3. **Observe for Deviation**:
   - Once you have a baseline, pay attention to sudden, brief expressions when you ask emotionally or factually significant questions. These micro-expressions could indicate concealed emotions.

4. **Interpret the Expression**:
   - Refer to known micro-expressions:
     - Tightening of lips might indicate discomfort or anger.
     - A quick eyebrow raise could signal surprise or doubt.
     - A flash of a smile that disappears quickly might indicate sarcasm or insincerity.

5. **Respond Accordingly**:
   - If you catch a micro-expression indicating discomfort, adjust your questioning to explore the area further. If you see signs of anger, remain calm and neutral, allowing the person to reveal more.

Adapting to Sensory Feedback: Shifts in Body Language and Behavior

Body Language: The Unspoken Response

Beyond facial expressions, shifts in body language—such as changes in posture, hand movements, or breathing patterns—offer critical information about how someone is reacting. In a courtroom, these subtle shifts can signal whether a witness is uncomfortable, a juror is engaged or disinterested, or if opposing counsel is becoming nervous.

The Lawyer Who Noticed the Shift

During voir dire, attorney Michael was questioning a potential juror about their opinion on self-defense cases. The juror responded verbally in support of self-defense, but Michael noticed a slight leaning away from him and a subtle crossing of the arms—non-verbal cues indicating discomfort or disinterest. Sensing this discrepancy, Michael adjusted his approach, asking more open-ended questions to explore the juror's true feelings. Eventually, the juror admitted their reluctance to support self-defense claims, allowing Michael to challenge their inclusion on the jury.

Step-by-Step Guide: Calibrating Body Language

1. **Establish a Neutral Baseline**:
   - Begin by observing the individual when they are not under stress. Notice their typical posture, breathing, and gestures. This baseline will help you detect any deviations later.
2. **Observe Subtle Shifts During Questioning**:
   - Watch for changes such as leaning forward (indicating interest), leaning back (disengagement or skepticism), or crossing arms (defensiveness). These shifts reveal how the person is reacting to your questions.
3. **Interpret the Signals**:
   - If a witness leans back when asked a specific question, it might indicate discomfort. If they suddenly start fidgeting or breathing faster, it could signal anxiety or nervousness.
4. **Adapt Your Approach Based on Feedback**:
   - If you detect defensiveness, soften your tone or shift to a less confrontational line of questioning to put the witness at ease.
   - If you observe engagement (e.g., a juror leans forward when you make a point), amplify that by emphasizing related details to maintain their interest.

5. **Re-Calibrate as Needed**:
   - o Continuously observe and adjust as you receive new sensory feedback. For example, if you notice a shift from engagement to disinterest in a juror, shift your focus or adjust your delivery to re-engage them.

Advanced Techniques: Sensory Acuity in Action

Calibration and Sensory Acuity Across Legal Scenarios

1. **Witness Cross-Examination**:
   - o During cross-examination, calibrate the witness's reactions to your questions. If they display sudden tension, such as a tightening jaw or hands clenching, these are signals of discomfort. Adjust by probing further into the topic to create pressure, increasing the likelihood that the witness reveals more.
2. **Voir Dire (Jury Selection)**:
   - o Use calibration during voir dire to gauge juror responses. Ask jurors about their feelings on certain legal issues and observe their micro-expressions and body language. Those who lean away or display fleeting expressions of discomfort may not be suitable jurors for your case.
3. **Motion Hearings**:
   - o When presenting arguments in motion hearings, observe the judge's reactions. Subtle cues like nodding, leaning forward, or frowning provide sensory feedback on whether your argument is being well-received. Calibrate your responses accordingly to align with the judge's apparent interest or concern.
4. **Negotiations with Opposing Counsel**:

o During settlement negotiations, use calibration to sense when opposing counsel may be bluffing or feeling pressured. If they start avoiding eye contact or show tension (e.g., clenching fists or shifting posture), this may indicate vulnerability. Adapt by pressing further on your terms or shifting to a more conciliatory approach, depending on your objectives.

Practical Scripts: Employing Calibration Techniques

1. **Establishing the Baseline with a Witness**:
   o "Thank you for your time today. Can you tell me how long you've known the defendant?" *(Observe the witness's neutral behavior as a baseline.)*
2. **Calibrating During Cross-Examination**:
   o "Now, you mentioned that you were certain of the time you saw the event. Can you confirm that it was exactly 6 PM?" *(If the witness's body language changes, such as shifting posture or breaking eye contact, note this deviation as a sign of discomfort or uncertainty.)*
3. **Engaging Jurors During Voir Dire**:
   o "Do you believe that everyone deserves a fair defense, regardless of the charges?" *(Observe the juror's body language—leaning forward or maintaining eye contact signals engagement, while crossing arms or looking away suggests defensiveness or disagreement.)*

Mastering Calibration and Sensory Acuity for Legal Success

Calibration and sensory acuity are powerful tools for any attorney seeking to gain an advantage in the courtroom. By observing micro-expressions and body language, attorneys can gauge real-time emotional and cognitive states, allowing them to adapt their strategies and enhance their influence.

Whether examining witnesses, selecting jurors, or negotiating with opposing counsel, mastering these techniques ensures that attorneys remain perceptive and responsive, turning subtle, often overlooked cues into critical insights that shape outcomes.

Pattern Interrupts and Reset Techniques: Regaining Control When Testimony Goes Off Track

In the courtroom, there are moments when a witness becomes uncooperative, combative, or overly defensive, making it difficult to extract the desired information or maintain control of the examination. Pattern interrupts and reset techniques are powerful strategies that allow attorneys to disrupt these unhelpful patterns and reestablish control over the direction of the testimony. By using subtle movements, shifts in questioning, or changes in tone, attorneys can break the rhythm of a witness's behavior, resetting the interaction and guiding it back to a productive path. This section explores the intricacies of these techniques, providing practical examples and scripts to illustrate their application.

Understanding Pattern Interrupts: Breaking the Cycle of Resistance

What Are Pattern Interrupts? The Science of Disruption

Pattern interrupts involve breaking the flow of an established behavior or response pattern. In the context of the courtroom, this can mean disrupting a witness's repetitive answers, evasive tactics, or defensive posture. By doing so, the attorney forces the witness out of their automatic response mode, making them more receptive to new questions or lines of inquiry.

The concept is grounded in psychology and NLP: when a pattern is disrupted, the brain briefly pauses to reassess the situation, creating a moment of openness where the attorney can redirect the witness's focus. This technique is particularly effective when dealing with witnesses who seem well-rehearsed or overly confident, as it introduces an element of unpredictability that can make them more vulnerable to revealing inconsistencies.

The Attorney Who Mastered the Art of the Pattern Interrupt

During a cross-examination in a high-profile fraud case, defense attorney Lisa faced a witness who consistently responded with vague, rehearsed statements. Each time she probed for specifics, the witness repeated the same defensive phrases, making it difficult for her to gain any meaningful traction. Sensing the pattern, Lisa decided to employ a pattern interrupt. She paused, adjusted her posture by leaning in slightly, and then asked an unrelated, surprising question: "By the way, could you remind me of the street name where you said you work?" The sudden shift caught the witness off guard, causing them to stumble momentarily. In that brief window of uncertainty, Lisa quickly pivoted back to her original line of questioning. The witness, now off-balance, hesitated, providing more detail than they had initially intended.

Step-by-Step Guide: Implementing Pattern Interrupts

1. **Recognize the Pattern**:
   - Identify when the witness is falling into repetitive behavior, such as repeating phrases, dodging questions, or becoming defensive.
2. **Introduce an Unexpected Element**:
   - This could be a subtle shift in your tone, a sudden pause, a change in posture (e.g., leaning

forward or folding your hands), or an unexpected question that briefly disrupts the witness's focus.

3. **Create a Moment of Confusion**:
   o The goal is to introduce an element that is just unfamiliar enough to make the witness pause and reassess the situation. This momentary confusion opens the door for you to redirect the questioning.

4. **Pivot Back to the Original Line of Inquiry**:
   o Once you have disrupted the pattern, quickly return to your key question. The interruption should make the witness less confident, making them more likely to provide a genuine response.

5. **Reinforce Control Through Tone and Body Language**:
   o After the pattern interrupt, maintain a confident and controlled demeanor. This reinforces your authority in the situation, making it clear to the witness and the jury that you are in command of the proceedings.

Practical Application: Using Pattern Interrupts Across Legal Scenarios

1. **Cross-Examination of Witnesses**:
   o When a witness becomes evasive or defensive, use a pattern interrupt such as pausing for an extended moment, then shifting the questioning to an unrelated but relevant detail (e.g., "What color was the car you drove that day?"). This brief departure disrupts their focus and prepares them for a return to the original question with reduced resistance.

2. **Negotiations with Opposing Counsel**:
   o In negotiations, if opposing counsel repeats the same stance or argument, use a pattern interrupt by changing the topic momentarily (e.g., "Before we proceed, I noticed something

interesting in the case file—can we discuss that first?"). This disrupts their flow, providing a chance to reset the conversation.

3. **Motion Hearings**:
   - When a judge seems unresponsive to your argument, subtly adjust your delivery—either by slowing down your speech or changing your posture—to break the pattern of their disinterest. This creates a moment of renewed attention, allowing you to emphasize your point with added impact.

4. **Engaging Jurors**:
   - During opening statements, if you sense jurors losing focus, introduce a pattern interrupt by posing a rhetorical question or pausing to shift eye contact with individual jurors. This can break their inattentiveness, re-engaging them with your narrative.

Reset Techniques: Bringing the Interaction Back on Track

The Art of the Reset: Regaining Control in Tense Situations

While pattern interrupts break the cycle, reset techniques focus on re-establishing a productive and controlled environment. This is essential when interactions become tense, either because the witness becomes combative or the questioning escalates emotionally. Reset techniques use subtle movements, verbal cues, or tone adjustments to de-escalate the situation, regain composure, and guide the interaction back to a constructive path.

The Lawyer Who Used a Reset Technique to Regain Control

Defense attorney Mark was questioning a witness who became increasingly agitated, raising their voice and interrupting his questions. Mark could see that the witness's emotional state was creating a tense atmosphere, making it difficult to proceed effectively. Instead of pushing back immediately, Mark employed a reset technique. He paused, took a slow breath, and calmly adjusted his posture by sitting back and folding his hands on the desk. This non-verbal cue signaled a shift in energy, diffusing the tension. He then lowered his voice and said, "Let's take a moment to clarify—we're here to understand the facts." The witness mirrored his calm demeanor, and the atmosphere of the examination shifted, allowing Mark to regain control.

Step-by-Step Guide: Applying Reset Techniques

1. **Identify the Escalation**:
   o Recognize when the interaction is becoming tense or when the witness is showing signs of agitation (e.g., raised voice, quickened speech, or aggressive posture).
2. **Create a Pause**:
   o Take a brief pause before responding. This allows you to reset your own emotional state and signals to the witness and the jury that you are maintaining control.
3. **Adjust Your Posture or Tone**:
   o Change your body language (e.g., lean back, fold your hands, or sit upright) or adjust your tone to a calmer, slower pace. This signals a reset in the energy of the exchange and often encourages the other person to mirror your behavior.
4. **Reframe the Situation**:
   o Use a phrase like, "Let's take a step back," or "I understand this is a sensitive topic—let's work through it calmly." This verbal cue reinforces the

physical reset, creating a structured opportunity for the interaction to de-escalate.

5. **Guide the Witness Back to the Focus**:
    o Once the tension has decreased, pivot back to your key question or line of inquiry, maintaining a calm, steady demeanor to reinforce your control.

Practical Application: Using Reset Techniques Across Legal Scenarios

1. **Cross-Examination**:
    o When a witness becomes defensive or emotional, pause, take a breath, and adjust your posture. Use a phrase like, "I appreciate your honesty— let's revisit the details slowly." This reset can calm the witness and create an environment conducive to getting the information you need.
2. **Motion Hearings and Trial Arguments**:
    o If the judge becomes visibly frustrated or inattentive, reset the tone by lowering your voice and slowing down your pace. Acknowledging the importance of clarity (e.g., "I understand this is a complex point, Your Honor; allow me to clarify") can create space for re-engagement.
3. **Jury Interactions During Closing Arguments**:
    o If you notice jurors losing focus, employ a reset by briefly pausing, making eye contact with different jurors, and transitioning with a slower, deliberate statement: "Let's reflect on what we've discussed so far..." This draws their attention back and re-engages them in your argument.

Practical Scripts: Employing Pattern Interrupts and Reset Techniques

1. **Pattern Interrupt During Witness Cross-Examination**:

- "You mentioned you were absolutely certain about the time. Before we continue, what street were you walking on that day?" *(This change disrupts the witness's rhythm, opening a window to reset the questioning.)*

2. **Reset Technique When the Witness Becomes Agitated**:
   - "I can see this is a sensitive subject. Let's take a moment, and we'll go through it step by step." *(Pausing and changing tone to a calm, slower pace helps to de-escalate the situation.)*

3. **Pattern Interrupt with Opposing Counsel in Negotiation**:
   - "Before we move forward, could we take a moment to review the section on witness credibility again?" *(The shift in topic disrupts opposing counsel's flow, creating an opportunity to reset the discussion.)*

Mastering Pattern Interrupts and Reset Techniques for Legal Control

Pattern interrupts and reset techniques are essential tools for attorneys who want to maintain control and authority in the courtroom. By breaking unproductive patterns and resetting the tone of tense interactions, attorneys can redirect testimony, manage witness behavior, and effectively engage with jurors, judges, and opposing counsel. Mastering these techniques ensures that attorneys can navigate even the most challenging scenarios with composure and strategic precision, turning moments of tension into opportunities for influence.

As we move into the critical realm of managing juror perceptions and emotions, the focus shifts to understanding how non-verbal communication, storytelling, and strategic reframing can shape a jury's interpretation of a case. In this section, we explore the subtle art of influencing jurors through body language, synchronizing with their energy levels to maintain their attention, and crafting narratives that resonate with their values. Additionally, we delve into the power of metaphors and reframing techniques that transform potentially damaging evidence into neutral or even favorable elements. These strategies provide attorneys with the tools to connect with jurors on a deeper level, ensuring they remain engaged, receptive, and aligned with the intended message throughout the trial.

6. The Art of Juror Influence: Techniques for Shaping Perceptions and Emotions

In a trial, the jury's perception of the case can often be the deciding factor between conviction and acquittal. Effectively managing juror perceptions and emotions requires a nuanced blend of non-verbal communication, storytelling, and strategic reframing. This section delves into advanced techniques designed to create rapport with jurors, influence their focus, and guide their understanding of the case. From using body language to synchronize with juror energy levels, to crafting compelling narratives and metaphors that resonate with their values, and finally, to reframing evidence in ways that shift perspectives—these methods equip attorneys with the skills needed to connect with jurors on both intellectual and emotional levels, ensuring their message lands with maximum impact.

Non-Verbal Rapport Techniques for Jurors: Building Trust Without Words

Establishing rapport with jurors is one of the most powerful yet subtle tools in a trial lawyer's arsenal. Non-verbal rapport techniques enable attorneys to influence jurors' perception and focus through body language alone, creating a silent connection that fosters trust and engagement. By synchronizing body language with jurors' energy levels, attorneys can guide attention, reinforce key points, and create an atmosphere where jurors are more receptive to the presented arguments. This section explores techniques for achieving this non-verbal influence, offering step-by-step instructions and practical strategies tailored to trial scenarios.

Silent Influence: Communicating Without Words

Body Language as a Tool for Building Trust

Body language, though silent, is one of the most influential aspects of communication, especially in the courtroom, where jurors are watching every move an attorney makes. An attorney's posture, gestures, and even their breathing rate can send signals of confidence, empathy, and credibility—qualities that jurors intuitively seek in someone they can trust. By understanding how body language affects perception, attorneys can subtly align with jurors' subconscious expectations, fostering a sense of rapport that makes jurors more receptive.

The Lawyer Who Connected Through Body Language

Consider defense attorney Julia, who noticed during a high-stakes criminal trial that some jurors seemed distant, occasionally glancing away during her closing statements. Rather than pushing her points verbally, Julia decided to adjust her body language to engage them on a subconscious level. She mirrored the jurors' postures—leaning slightly forward when they did, softening her facial expressions, and nodding subtly when making eye contact. Gradually, the jurors began to reflect her posture and gestures, unconsciously mirroring her as well. By the end of the closing, they were more engaged and receptive, leaning forward with intent and maintaining eye contact. Julia's non-verbal connection created a silent rapport that supported her verbal arguments, ultimately helping sway the verdict.

Step-by-Step Guide: Influencing Jurors Through Body Language

1. **Begin with Open, Confident Posture**:

- Stand with feet shoulder-width apart and avoid crossing arms. This open stance signals confidence and accessibility to jurors.

2. **Mirror Juror Postures Subtly**:
   - Observe individual jurors' body language. If a juror leans forward, match their posture by subtly leaning forward as you speak, signaling a shared level of engagement.

3. **Use Consistent Eye Contact**:
   - Maintain steady eye contact with different jurors for brief moments, giving each juror a sense of individualized attention. This non-verbal interaction builds trust and keeps them engaged.

4. **Gesture Naturally and in Synchrony with Your Words**:
   - Use open-handed gestures when emphasizing points, as this conveys honesty. Keep gestures steady and purposeful, as rushed or exaggerated movements can signal nervousness or insincerity.

5. **Use Pauses to Emphasize and Invite Reflection**:
   - Pausing while maintaining eye contact draws attention to key moments in your statement, allowing jurors to absorb your message and reinforcing its importance.

Practical Application: Body Language Techniques for Trial Scenarios

1. **Opening Statements**:
   - In opening statements, begin with an open posture and consistent eye contact with each juror. Use slow, deliberate gestures that match the rhythm of your speech to establish authority and confidence from the outset.

2. **Cross-Examination**:
   - Use subtle body language shifts to maintain rapport with the jury while cross-examining a witness. When asking critical questions, make

eye contact with jurors briefly, allowing them to feel included and reinforcing the importance of the question.

3. **Closing Arguments**:
   o In closing arguments, mirror the body language of jurors who appear most engaged. Subtly leaning forward or nodding in sync with them can create a sense of alignment, making your arguments feel more personal and compelling.

Synchronizing with Jury Energy Levels: The Rhythm of Rapport

The Subtle Art of Synchronization

An attorney's ability to align with jurors' energy levels throughout the trial can be crucial for maintaining their attention and focus. Synchronization involves gauging the energy of the room and adapting your pace, tone, and movements to match it, creating a natural flow that keeps jurors engaged. If jurors appear fatigued or unfocused, slowing down or using a quieter tone can bring them back into alignment. Conversely, if jurors are highly attentive, increasing energy or pacing can capitalize on their engagement. This rhythm of rapport ensures that jurors stay attuned to the attorney's message.

The Attorney Who Mastered Synchronization

During a long and complex fraud trial, attorney Leo noticed jurors were beginning to look weary after several hours of witness testimony. To regain their attention, Leo adjusted his approach: he slowed his speaking pace, used softer tones, and incorporated brief pauses. This change in rhythm subtly drew jurors back in, as they instinctively matched his slower pace and began focusing on his words with renewed attention. By the time Leo finished his examination, the jurors appeared more alert, nodding occasionally in response to his statements. His skillful synchronization helped reset the jurors' focus, preparing them for the next critical segment of the trial.

Step-by-Step Guide: Synchronizing with Jury Energy Levels

1. **Gauge the Room's Energy Level**:
   - Observe jurors' body language. Signs of fatigue include slumped posture, fidgeting, or looking away, while upright posture and leaning forward suggest engagement.
2. **Adapt Your Voice and Pace**:
   - If jurors appear fatigued, soften your tone and slow your pace. If they are highly engaged, speak with increased energy and quicker pacing to maintain their attention.
3. **Adjust Posture and Movements to Match the Energy**:
   - In moments of high engagement, use more animated gestures and a more assertive posture to capitalize on the energy. During quieter moments, maintain a calm, steady stance with minimal movement.
4. **Use Pauses to Reset Attention**:
   - In moments of waning focus, employ a pause to break the rhythm. This unexpected silence brings jurors' attention back to you, creating an opportunity to re-establish focus.
5. **Re-Energize Through Subtle Shifts**:
   - If the energy remains low, consider briefly shifting topics or using a rhetorical question to invite curiosity. This change acts as a pattern interrupt, helping to recapture jurors' attention.

Practical Scripts: Applying Synchronization Techniques with Jurors

1. **During a Lengthy Examination**:

- o "Now, let's take a moment to consider..." *(Use a pause here while making eye contact with the jurors, signaling a shift in focus and giving them a moment to re-engage.)*
2. **In Closing Arguments**:
   - o "As we bring all the facts together..." *(Slow down your pace and soften your tone here if jurors seem fatigued, allowing them to recalibrate their attention.)*
3. **During Voir Dire**:
   - o "I understand that this process may seem lengthy..." *(Acknowledge the jury's experience and adjust your energy to match theirs, showing empathy and respect for their time and focus.)*

Advanced Strategies: Combining Body Language and Synchronization for Maximum Impact

The Power of Mirroring and Synchronization in Tandem

The most effective attorneys combine mirroring and synchronization to create a powerful sense of rapport with jurors. By subtly matching jurors' postures and energy levels, attorneys can create a state of alignment that feels authentic and trustworthy. For example, during emotionally intense testimony, an attorney who matches jurors' solemnity and paces their statements with empathy can create a shared experience that strengthens rapport. This approach ensures jurors feel emotionally connected to the narrative, enhancing the persuasiveness of the attorney's arguments.

Adapting Techniques in Real-Time

An essential skill in courtroom communication is adaptability. Non-verbal rapport techniques and synchronization are most effective when applied dynamically, based on jurors' real-time reactions. Practicing sensory acuity—watching for subtle changes in jurors' expressions or posture—enables attorneys to adjust their approach as needed, ensuring they remain in sync with jurors' emotions and focus levels.

Mastering Non-Verbal Rapport and Synchronization for Jury Engagement

Non-verbal rapport techniques and synchronization are foundational tools for trial attorneys seeking to connect with jurors on a subconscious level. By influencing jurors through body language and aligning with their energy levels, attorneys can foster a silent connection that enhances receptivity and focus. Mastering these techniques allows attorneys to navigate the courtroom with subtlety and skill, turning jurors from passive observers into engaged participants who feel aligned with the attorney's message. This alignment is key to maintaining influence, guiding perceptions, and ultimately shaping the outcome of a trial.

Storytelling and Metaphor Techniques: Engaging Jurors on a Personal Level

In the courtroom, logic and evidence are essential, but they alone rarely capture jurors' hearts and minds. Effective attorneys know that storytelling and metaphors are powerful tools for building empathy, creating memorable connections, and guiding jurors toward specific conclusions. By crafting compelling narratives and using metaphors that align with jurors' values, attorneys can make complex legal arguments relatable and understandable, increasing the likelihood of a favorable verdict. This section delves into advanced storytelling techniques, offering insights into constructing narratives and choosing metaphors that resonate deeply with jurors' perspectives.

The Power of Storytelling: Transforming Facts into a Journey

Why Stories Work: The Psychology of Engagement

Stories have a profound impact on the human mind because they engage the brain on an emotional level. Unlike mere facts, stories activate multiple areas of the brain—such as those responsible for sensory processing, emotional engagement, and memory retention—making information more vivid and easier to recall. In a trial setting, storytelling enables jurors to visualize the events, empathize with the individuals involved, and understand the context beyond the facts.

The Attorney Who Used Storytelling to Shift Perspective

Consider the case of defense attorney Daniel, who represented a client charged with a non-violent theft. To engage the jury, Daniel crafted a story that went beyond the defendant's actions and delved into the circumstances that led to the alleged crime. He began his closing argument with, "Imagine you're a father struggling to make ends meet, working long hours just to keep a roof over your family's head." He continued, describing the difficult choices his client faced. This narrative allowed jurors to empathize with the defendant as a human being, not merely as a case number. By the end, jurors had a clearer, more compassionate view of the defendant, leading to a more favorable verdict.

Step-by-Step Guide: Crafting Compelling Narratives for Jurors

1. **Begin with a Relatable Premise**:
   o Identify the core values or emotions in your case, such as justice, family, or personal hardship.

145

Start your story with a premise that jurors can relate to, making it easier for them to connect emotionally.

2. **Introduce a Protagonist with Clear Motivations**:
   o Position your client, the victim, or even a witness as the protagonist of the story. Describe their motivations, challenges, and actions to humanize them and create empathy.

3. **Build Tension with Specific Details**:
   o Use vivid details to paint a picture of the circumstances. This might include sensory descriptions (e.g., the sound of heavy footsteps, the feeling of a tight grip) to make the story immersive.

4. **Guide Jurors Toward a Resolution**:
   o Conclude the narrative by reinforcing the desired perspective, whether it's to evoke sympathy, highlight an injustice, or underscore the importance of reasonable doubt.

5. **Reinforce Key Themes**:
   o Throughout the narrative, subtly reinforce the themes that support your argument, such as resilience, integrity, or accountability. These themes will resonate with jurors, influencing their perception of the case.

Practical Application: Storytelling Techniques for Legal Scenarios

1. **Opening Statements**:
   o In opening statements, start with a story that frames the case from your client's perspective. For example, in a self-defense case, "Picture yourself alone at night, hearing footsteps behind you, your heart racing..." This invites jurors to step into the client's experience, setting the tone for a sympathetic understanding.

2. **Cross-Examination**:

- o Use storytelling to challenge a witness's credibility by drawing attention to inconsistencies in their account. For instance, "Let's revisit that night. You said you left at 8:00, yet you recall the streetlights coming on. Isn't that unusual?"

3. **Closing Arguments**:
   - o In your closing argument, weave together the key facts into a cohesive story that reinforces your case's theme. Reiterate key moments from testimonies or evidence, linking them into a narrative that supports your interpretation of events.

The Art of Metaphors: Making the Abstract Relatable

Why Metaphors Work: Connecting with Jurors' Values

Metaphors are a powerful linguistic tool for simplifying complex ideas by comparing them to familiar concepts. In a trial, metaphors can help jurors grasp legal principles, understand evidence, or view your client in a favorable light. The key to effective metaphor use is aligning with values and experiences that resonate with the jurors, creating a bridge between the legal complexities and the jurors' everyday understanding.

The Lawyer Who Used Metaphors to Simplify a Case

Attorney Sarah represented a client accused of negligence in a workplace accident. Knowing the jurors might find the technical aspects overwhelming, she employed a metaphor: "Imagine a ship's captain steering through a storm. If they hit an unexpected wave, it doesn't mean they weren't doing their best to steer safely." This metaphor helped jurors understand the concept of unforeseen circumstances, making it easier to see her client's actions as reasonable rather than negligent. By the end of her closing, the metaphor had reframed the case in the client's favor.

Step-by-Step Guide: Crafting and Using Effective Metaphors

1. **Identify the Core Message**:
   - Decide on the concept you want to simplify, whether it's "reasonable doubt," "burden of proof," or the challenges your client faced. This will help guide your choice of metaphor.
2. **Choose a Familiar, Relatable Concept**:
   - Select a metaphor that aligns with common juror experiences, like "steering a ship," "following a recipe," or "building a puzzle." These familiar ideas make the abstract concept feel intuitive.
3. **Ensure the Metaphor Reinforces Your Argument**:
   - Test the metaphor to make sure it doesn't inadvertently support the opposing argument. For example, using "steering a ship" conveys control and caution, which reinforces a defense of responsible behavior.
4. **Integrate the Metaphor Naturally into Testimony or Arguments**:
   - Weave the metaphor seamlessly into your statements. Instead of explicitly stating, "This is like steering a ship," embed it: "Like any captain facing a storm, my client made the best choices they could."
5. **Revisit the Metaphor at Key Moments**:
   - Reiterate the metaphor at strategic points, such as during cross-examination or closing arguments, to reinforce its connection to your case's themes and anchor jurors' understanding.

Practical Application: Using Metaphors in Legal Scenarios

1. **During Voir Dire**:
   o Use metaphors to connect with potential jurors and explain legal principles. For example, "Just like building a house, finding the truth here requires us to carefully lay each brick of evidence." This primes jurors for a methodical examination of facts.
2. **Explaining Evidence in Motion Hearings**:
   o When discussing technical evidence, use metaphors to simplify complex concepts. In a forensic case, for instance, "Think of DNA testing as piecing together a puzzle, where each piece tells us something about the whole picture."
3. **Clarifying Legal Principles in Closing**:
   o Use metaphors to reinforce the principle of reasonable doubt, such as: "Deciding a case is like painting a portrait. If there are blank spaces that can't be filled, then the picture is incomplete, and doubt remains."

Advanced Strategies: Combining Storytelling and Metaphors

Blending Narrative and Metaphor for Maximum Impact

The most effective courtroom presentations often combine storytelling and metaphor, creating an immersive experience that is both emotionally and intellectually engaging. For example, an attorney might open with a story that mirrors a metaphor used later in the closing argument, creating continuity that reinforces the case's themes. This blend can heighten the emotional impact of your narrative, making it memorable and persuasive.

Reframing Evidence with Story and Metaphor

When evidence could be perceived as unfavorable, reframing it within a story or metaphor can neutralize its impact. For instance, in a case where a client's financial hardship might look suspicious, an attorney might use the metaphor of a "tightrope walker," emphasizing the precarious balance and difficult choices rather than suggesting irresponsibility. This reframing allows jurors to empathize, turning a potential liability into a relatable challenge.

Practical Script: Storytelling and Metaphor Techniques in Action

1. **Opening Statement Story**:
   - "Imagine stepping into a situation where every decision feels like a choice between two impossible outcomes... This is where my client found himself on that day, trying to balance what was right with what he believed to be safe."
2. **Metaphor During Cross-Examination**:
   - "So, would you say that in managing the situation, my client was like a captain in a storm, trying to steer through conditions beyond his control?"
3. **Reframing in Closing Argument**:
   - "Remember that blank spaces don't make a complete portrait. Just as a missing puzzle piece leaves the picture unfinished, gaps in the evidence leave us with questions that we can't ignore."

Harnessing Storytelling and Metaphors for Juror Engagement

Storytelling and metaphors are transformative techniques in trial advocacy, bridging the gap between complex legal arguments and jurors' everyday experiences. By crafting narratives that evoke empathy and using metaphors that simplify legal principles, attorneys can create compelling cases that jurors can grasp, remember, and align with on a personal level. When skillfully employed, these techniques can be the difference between an argument that is simply heard and one that is deeply felt, paving the way for jurors to reach the desired verdict with confidence and conviction.

Subtle Reframing Techniques: Shaping Jury Perception with Precision

In the courtroom, the way evidence is presented can be as powerful as the evidence itself. Reframing techniques allow attorneys to subtly adjust jurors' perceptions, shifting their understanding of facts and arguments to align with a more favorable interpretation. By carefully positioning unfavorable information, attorneys can minimize its impact, transforming potential weaknesses into neutral or even positive elements. This section explores the advanced skill of reframing in trial advocacy, offering insights into adjusting jury perception and turning problematic evidence into points of strength.

The Art of Reframing: Changing Perspectives, Not Facts

Why Reframing Works: Shifting Context Without Changing Content

Reframing changes the way jurors view facts, evidence, or testimony by altering the context around them. It relies on psychological principles, as jurors' perceptions are influenced by how information is framed. By subtly redirecting focus or reinterpreting implications, attorneys can steer jurors toward a more favorable understanding of the information without needing to alter or exclude any details.

The Defense Attorney Who Reframed Financial Hardship

Consider attorney Anna, representing a client in a theft case where financial hardship played a role. The prosecution highlighted the client's financial situation as evidence of motive, painting them as someone who would resort to theft. However, Anna reframed the situation, presenting her client as a person making honorable efforts to overcome adversity. She acknowledged the financial challenges but emphasized that her client had consistently worked to support his family. By reframing the hardship as evidence of resilience and responsibility, Anna turned what could have been seen as a motive for theft into a story of perseverance, inspiring empathy and casting doubt on the prosecution's narrative.

Step-by-Step Guide: Adjusting Jury Perception of Evidence

1. **Identify the Potentially Unfavorable Fact**:
   o Examine the evidence, witness testimony, or argument that may create a negative perception and assess how jurors might interpret it.
2. **Determine the Desired Perspective**:
   o Decide on the alternative view you want jurors to adopt. This could be shifting from blame to empathy, from doubt to understanding, or from suspicion to reason.
3. **Find a Contextual Frame**:
   o Choose a frame that reshapes the perception. For example, if the evidence implies negligence, frame it as an honest mistake in a high-pressure situation rather than carelessness.
4. **Use Relatable Language and Analogies**:
   o Employ analogies or relatable terms to make the reframe accessible. For instance, if a client made a rushed decision, compare it to a split-second

choice jurors might make in their own lives, encouraging empathy.

5. **Reinforce the Reframe Subtly Throughout the Trial**:
   o Refer back to the reframe in statements, questioning, and closing arguments to strengthen the new perspective. This repetition ensures that jurors view the fact within the favorable frame consistently.

Practical Application: Reframing Techniques Across Legal Scenarios

1. **Cross-Examination of a Witness with Unfavorable Testimony**:
   o If a witness testifies about your client's presence at a contentious location, reframe by emphasizing your client's legitimate reasons for being there, casting doubt on the alleged intent.
2. **Opening Statements with Potentially Negative Evidence**:
   o Introduce potentially damaging evidence preemptively, but present it within a favorable frame. For example, "You'll hear about an event where my client made a difficult choice in a complex situation—decisions we all might struggle with under such circumstances."
3. **Motion Hearings with Challenging Evidence**:
   o When presenting a motion that includes problematic information, frame it in the broader context of procedural fairness or legal rights, encouraging the judge to prioritize these principles.

Techniques for Turning Unfavorable Facts into Neutral or Positive Points

Owning the Narrative: Conceding with Control

One of the most effective reframing techniques is to concede unfavorable facts but do so in a way that minimizes their impact. This method prevents opposing counsel from weaponizing the information by framing it first in your own terms.

The Lawyer Who Turned Neglect into Noble Effort

In a case involving a company accused of environmental negligence, the attorney acknowledged a delay in response to an environmental spill but reframed it as a consequence of the company's extensive checks to ensure safety. Instead of presenting the delay as negligence, the attorney highlighted the commitment to thorough evaluation and employee well-being. This reframe neutralized the impact of the delay, portraying it as evidence of responsibility rather than carelessness.

Step-by-Step Guide: Conceding Unfavorable Facts to Reframe

1. **Acknowledge the Fact Early**:
   - Bring up the potentially damaging fact before the opposition has a chance, showing confidence and control.
2. **Present a Favorable Interpretation**:
   - Offer a favorable context, such as explaining the rationale behind a decision. For instance, if evidence shows a client was hesitant, frame it as a thoughtful approach rather than indecisiveness.
3. **Position the Fact as Evidence of a Positive Trait**:

- Link the fact to a positive characteristic, like responsibility or integrity, reinforcing that interpretation.
4. **Use Language that Reduces Emotional Impact**:
   - Choose neutral terms to discuss the fact. For example, say "careful consideration" instead of "delay," which minimizes emotional bias.

Advanced Reframing Strategies for Maximizing Impact

Using Contrast for Emphasis

Contrast is a powerful tool for reframing that involves comparing the unfavorable fact to a more relatable or less severe scenario, making the original fact seem less significant. By positioning the fact alongside a parallel that jurors understand, the attorney can downplay its impact.

Example: Reframing Intent with Contrast

In a fraud case, an attorney might compare the client's actions to a common, innocuous mistake, saying, "Just like when we balance our own checkbooks and miss an entry or two, honest errors can happen, especially under complex circumstances." This comparison shifts the focus from malicious intent to human error, reducing the perceived severity of the action.

Step-by-Step Guide: Using Contrast in Reframing

1. **Select an Appropriate Comparison**:
   - Choose a parallel situation that jurors can relate to, preferably something that minimizes the severity of the action in question.
2. **Highlight the Differences in Stakes or Intent**:
   - Emphasize that while the actions may be similar, the intent or circumstances were different,

reinforcing the idea that the behavior was unintentional or understandable.

3. **Reinforce the Reframe with Subtle Language**:
   o Use phrases like "Just as we…" or "Similar to when…" to reinforce the analogy, encouraging jurors to see the fact through a more forgiving lens.

Practical Scripts: Reframing Techniques in Action

1. **Opening Statement Reframe**:
   o "You will hear about an action my client took under incredibly stressful circumstances. While it might seem hasty at first glance, consider the pressure they faced, much like any of us would feel in a moment where the stakes are high and time is short."
2. **Reframe During Cross-Examination**:
   o "So, you mentioned that my client hesitated in making a decision. Would you say that careful decision-making, especially when someone's reputation is on the line, is actually a responsible approach?"
3. **Closing Argument Contrast Reframe**:
   o "We all make decisions every day with the information we have at the moment. Just as we sometimes look back and think, 'I would have done it differently,' my client made the best decision they could under the circumstances. Hindsight is clear, but it doesn't change the integrity of their actions at that time."

Mastering Subtle Reframing for Juror Influence

Reframing techniques are essential tools for influencing juror perceptions and shifting focus toward favorable interpretations. By reshaping the context of potentially damaging information, attorneys can control the narrative, turning weaknesses into neutral or even positive elements. Through strategies like conceding with control, using contrast, and positioning facts within relatable frames, attorneys empower jurors to see the case from a more empathetic and aligned perspective. Mastering these techniques ensures that the jury interprets the evidence in a way that supports a compelling, credible, and persuasive defense.

As we shift our focus to witness examination, we explore the nuanced techniques that enable attorneys to extract clear, credible, and persuasive testimony while maintaining control over the narrative. Effective witness examination requires a blend of rapport-building, strategic questioning, and subtle influence. In direct examination, fostering trust and encouraging alignment are essential for a smooth, compelling testimony. Cross-examination, however, demands a different skill set—one that involves managing uncooperative or rehearsed witnesses by subtly disarming them and controlling the pace of questioning. Finally, we'll delve into advanced persuasion techniques, such as embedding suggestions and using pacing to shape witness responses and behavior. These methods give attorneys the tools to guide witness testimony with precision, ensuring that each statement aligns with the broader case strategy.

7. Mastering Witness Examination: Techniques for Influence and Control

Witness examination is a pivotal part of trial advocacy, where each question, response, and subtle cue can impact the jurors' perception of the facts. This section examines the art of guiding witness testimony with finesse and control, from building rapport and maintaining alignment in direct examination to managing challenging witnesses in cross-examination. We'll explore methods for establishing quick trust, using positive reinforcement, and leveraging advanced influence techniques like embedding suggestions and pacing to subtly shape a witness's responses. With these strategies, attorneys can direct witness narratives effectively, ensuring that each testimony strengthens the case while resonating with jurors.

Direct Examination Techniques: Building Trust and Reinforcing Alignment

Direct examination sets the stage for witness testimony, establishing the facts of the case in a clear and compelling way. For jurors, it's often their first impression of a witness, making it essential that the witness appears credible, aligned, and comfortable. Building trust and rapport quickly during direct examination is a powerful way to encourage the witness to relax and speak confidently, ensuring their testimony supports your case. Additionally, using positive reinforcement can help maintain alignment and confidence, encouraging the witness to stay focused and consistent throughout their testimony.

Creating Instant Rapport: The Foundation of Trust in Direct Examination

Why Rapport Matters: Setting the Tone for Credibility

Rapport is fundamental to successful direct examination because it fosters a connection between the attorney and the witness, allowing the testimony to flow smoothly and authentically. When rapport is established, the witness feels comfortable and supported, reducing the likelihood of nervousness or inconsistency. For jurors, rapport signals that the witness is trustworthy and aligned with the attorney's questions, promoting confidence in the testimony presented.

The Attorney Who Built Rapport to Strengthen Testimony

Consider attorney David, who was preparing a key witness for a case involving a car accident. The witness was visibly nervous, unsure about speaking in front of a jury. Sensing this, David began the direct examination with a few non-intimidating questions to help the witness settle in: "Could you tell us a bit about yourself and how long you've lived in this area?" This question was straightforward and allowed the witness to speak comfortably. With each question, David mirrored the witness's pace and tone, subtly nodding to reinforce trust. By the time David moved to more critical questions, the witness was calm, clear, and able to deliver testimony that resonated with the jury, helping the case tremendously.

Step-by-Step Guide: Building Rapport with a Witness During Direct Examination

1. **Start with Personal, Non-Threatening Questions**:

- Open the examination with simple questions that allow the witness to speak about familiar topics. These could include their background or general context of their involvement, providing a gentle entry into the examination.

2. **Mirror Body Language and Tone**:
   - Subtly match the witness's posture, gestures, and speech patterns. This creates a non-verbal connection that makes the witness feel supported and understood.

3. **Acknowledge and Validate Responses**:
   - Nod or respond with brief affirmations like "Thank you" or "I appreciate that." These gestures show that you're actively listening, helping the witness feel valued.

4. **Use Empathetic Language**:
   - Use phrases like "I understand" or "I know this may be difficult" to create a safe space for the witness, encouraging them to speak openly and confidently.

5. **Reassure When Necessary**:
   - If the witness appears nervous or hesitant, reassure them with a calm tone, saying, "Take your time." This helps reduce tension, ensuring their responses come through clearly.

Practical Application: Building Rapport Across Legal Scenarios

1. **Preparing a Nervous Witness in a Sensitive Case**:
   - Begin with easy questions that allow the witness to build confidence, such as asking about their background or role in the events. Once they're more relaxed, gradually transition to more specific topics relevant to the case.

2. **Examining an Expert Witness**:
   - With expert witnesses, rapport can be established by acknowledging their credentials and expertise upfront. This shows respect and

can make the witness feel validated, encouraging them to provide detailed, confident testimony.

3. **Motion Hearings with Complex Testimony**:
   - When examining a witness with technical information, start by confirming their expertise in their field. Simple questions like "Could you explain your role in this situation?" allow them to ease into the testimony, making the transition to complex topics smoother.

Positive Reinforcement: Keeping the Witness Aligned and Confident

The Psychology of Positive Reinforcement

Positive reinforcement strengthens desired behavior by rewarding it, making the witness more likely to stay aligned and focused throughout the examination. In the courtroom, this reinforcement encourages the witness to maintain a calm, cooperative, and consistent demeanor. Positive reinforcement also counters any nervousness or uncertainty the witness may feel, creating a feedback loop that boosts their confidence and willingness to engage.

The Lawyer Who Used Positive Reinforcement to Guide Testimony

During a high-profile fraud case, attorney Laura needed a witness to recall specific details about transactions. The witness was initially hesitant, unsure if they could remember every detail accurately. Laura used positive reinforcement to encourage the witness each time they provided clear, detailed answers. She nodded affirmatively, saying, "Thank you, that's helpful" after each answer. Gradually, the witness became more relaxed and confident, offering more specific information and aligning well with the case's narrative. By the end of the examination, Laura's reinforcement had encouraged the witness to share vital information that strengthened her client's position.

Step-by-Step Guide: Using Positive Reinforcement During Direct Examination

1. **Acknowledge Clear, Accurate Responses**:
   - After the witness provides a useful or clear answer, respond with affirmations like "Exactly" or "Thank you for clarifying." This feedback reassures them that they're on the right track.
2. **Show Subtle Approval Through Body Language**:
   - Use small gestures, such as nodding or leaning slightly forward, to signal your support and approval. This non-verbal reinforcement reinforces alignment without interrupting the flow.
3. **Use Encouraging Phrasing Between Questions**:
   - Between questions, use phrases like "You're doing great" or "That's very helpful" to keep the witness motivated and reassured, especially in high-stakes cases.
4. **Pause to Allow Processing and Build Confidence**:
   - After a challenging question, pause briefly to give the witness time to gather their thoughts. This shows you respect their process and encourages a thoughtful response.
5. **Repeat Key Points in Affirming Terms**:
   - If the witness provides an important detail, repeat it in your own words and add an affirming statement like "That's exactly what we needed to clarify." This reinforces their confidence in their response.

Practical Application: Positive Reinforcement Across Legal Scenarios

1. **Encouraging a Hesitant Witness During Examination**:
   o When a witness appears unsure, offer positive feedback for each correct or clear answer. For example, "That's exactly right. Your attention to detail is very helpful." This encourages them to stay focused and aligned with your line of questioning.
2. **Reinforcing Key Testimony with Jurors**:
   o After the witness provides a strong response that you want the jurors to remember, reinforce it with a phrase like "Thank you, that's an important detail." This not only boosts the witness's confidence but subtly emphasizes the point for the jury.
3. **Building Confidence During Calendar Negotiations**:
   o When preparing a witness for testimony, reinforce their confidence by acknowledging their effort and clarity in practice sessions. Statements like "You're well-prepared; the jury will appreciate your honesty" help reduce anxiety before the actual trial.

Advanced Strategies: Combining Rapport and Reinforcement for Maximum Impact

Creating a Loop of Positive Interaction

Combining rapport-building with positive reinforcement creates a continuous cycle that keeps the witness aligned and engaged throughout the testimony. For example, after establishing rapport with a witness through a relaxed and open introduction, positive reinforcement can be used after each response, reinforcing trust. This loop ensures that the witness feels supported, leading to a more consistent, credible testimony.

Using Repetition to Strengthen Key Testimony

Repetition, when combined with positive reinforcement, is a powerful tool to anchor important points. After a witness provides a critical answer, reinforcing the response with affirmations and subtly revisiting the point through subsequent questions reinforces its importance for both the witness and jurors, embedding it in their memory.

Practical Scripts: Direct Examination Techniques in Action

1. **Opening the Examination with Rapport**:
   o "Could you tell us a bit about yourself and your background in this area?" *(Gives the witness a comfortable starting point and establishes rapport)*
2. **Reinforcing Key Testimony**:
   o "Thank you, that's an important detail. Let's go over that again to make sure we fully understand." *(Uses positive reinforcement and repetition to strengthen key points)*
3. **Encouraging Confidence Mid-Examination**:
   o "You're doing great, take your time. Just let us know in your own words." *(Calms the witness, allowing them to respond with greater confidence)*

Mastering Direct Examination for Effective Witness Testimony

Direct examination is a crucial moment where attorneys can set a positive tone, encourage trust, and reinforce alignment between the witness's testimony and the case's strategy. By building rapport and using positive reinforcement, attorneys can guide witnesses to deliver confident, consistent, and credible testimony that resonates with jurors. Mastering these techniques ensures that witness examination is not just a transfer of information but an impactful, cohesive narrative that supports the case's core themes and builds juror confidence in the testimony provided.

Cross-Examination Techniques: Mastering Control and Disarming Hostility

Cross-examination is where attorneys test the credibility, accuracy, and reliability of a witness's statements. This part of witness examination is critical, especially when dealing with hostile or overly prepared witnesses who may attempt to undermine the questioning or steer the narrative in their favor. Successfully handling such witnesses requires finesse, control, and mastery of advanced techniques like mirroring, reframing, and tempo control. These tools empower attorneys to guide the questioning, maintain focus, and subtly influence the witness's responses, allowing the attorney to maintain authority while disarming any resistance.

Disarming Hostility: Using Mirroring and Reframing to Neutralize Resistance

Why Mirroring and Reframing Matter: Turning Conflict into Cooperation

Mirroring and reframing are powerful tools for managing uncooperative witnesses. Mirroring involves subtly reflecting a witness's body language, tone, or pace, creating an unconscious rapport that can make the witness more receptive. Reframing, on the other hand, involves reshaping the witness's responses or attitude to fit a different context, making their answers work in favor of your case. Together, these techniques disarm hostility, turn resistance into neutrality, and allow the attorney to maintain control over the flow of questioning.

The Attorney Who Used Mirroring to Disarm a Hostile Witness

Imagine attorney Sarah, who was cross-examining a key witness in a high-stakes corporate fraud case. The witness, visibly tense and defensive, frequently interrupted Sarah's questions and provided evasive responses. Sarah decided to use mirroring to subtly shift the energy. She adopted a calm tone, slowed her pace, and mirrored the witness's posture by leaning slightly forward. Over time, the witness unconsciously softened, reflecting Sarah's calm demeanor. Sarah then employed reframing by rephrasing the witness's statements, turning ambiguous answers into clear responses that favored her line of questioning. The witness, less defensive, gradually aligned with Sarah's controlled rhythm, allowing her to expose inconsistencies without confrontation.

Step-by-Step Guide: Disarming Hostility with Mirroring and Reframing

1. **Mirror the Witness's Body Language and Tone**:
   - Begin by observing the witness's physical stance, tone of voice, and pace of speech. Subtly match these elements to create a sense of familiarity without directly imitating them.
2. **Adjust Body Language as Needed**:
   - If the witness shows signs of nervousness or tension, mirror their body language initially, then gradually relax your posture. This often leads the witness to unconsciously match your calmer demeanor.
3. **Use Reframing to Clarify Evasive Responses**:
   - When the witness provides a vague or ambiguous answer, rephrase it in more precise terms. For example, if the witness says, "I think it was handled appropriately," respond with, "So, you're saying the procedure was followed exactly as required, correct?"

166

4. **Position Yourself as Cooperative**:
   - Frame your questions as if you're seeking clarity rather than challenging the witness. For example, "Just to make sure I understand..." or "Help me clarify..." lowers the witness's guard, making them more open to following your line of questioning.
5. **Introduce Positive Reframes When Hostility Emerges**:
   - If the witness becomes defensive, reframe their reaction as helpful. For instance, if they seem reluctant to answer, say, "I appreciate your thoughtful approach; I just want to ensure I have the full picture."

Practical Application: Using Mirroring and Reframing in Different Legal Scenarios

1. **Disarming During Cross-Examination**:
   - When a witness becomes defensive, use mirroring to match their intensity briefly, then gradually de-escalate. Pair this with reframing by rephrasing hostile responses as cooperative statements, shifting the tone from confrontation to collaboration.
2. **Handling a Prepared Witness in Motion Hearings**:
   - If the witness has rehearsed responses, mirror their formality initially to create rapport, then use reframing to challenge specific points. For example, "It sounds like you're confident about that process. Can we go over the specific details to ensure accuracy?"
3. **Reframing Witness Testimony During Jury Interactions**:
   - Reframe testimony in a way that aligns with jurors' values or understanding. For example, if a witness appears dismissive, reframe their statement to clarify the context, saying, "So, you

believe the standard process is thorough and reliable under normal circumstances?"

Controlling the Tempo: Guiding the Direction and Pacing of Questioning

Why Tempo Matters: Maintaining Command Without Confrontation

Controlling the pace and rhythm of cross-examination is crucial when handling witnesses who are prone to evasiveness or aggression. By adjusting the tempo—either speeding up to maintain focus or slowing down to emphasize key points—attorneys can subtly guide the witness's responses and prevent them from taking control of the exchange. This allows attorneys to highlight inconsistencies, avoid drawn-out answers, and keep jurors engaged.

The Attorney Who Mastered Tempo to Expose Inconsistencies

In a fraud trial, attorney Michael cross-examined a CFO who had rehearsed every answer. The witness responded with lengthy, complex statements, hoping to avoid direct questioning. To regain control, Michael began asking rapid-fire questions on specific details, preventing the witness from delivering rehearsed speeches. When he reached critical questions, Michael slowed his pace, enunciating each word, forcing the witness to consider every answer carefully. This tempo control left no room for evasiveness, exposing contradictions that proved pivotal to Michael's case.

Step-by-Step Guide: Controlling the Tempo and Direction of Questioning

1. **Establish a Baseline Tempo**:
    - Start with a moderate pace to observe how the witness naturally responds. Note whether they

speak slowly, quickly, or in long-winded answers, and adjust accordingly.

2. **Increase Tempo to Prevent Evasion**:
   - If the witness begins to offer extended or rehearsed answers, increase your pace by asking rapid, closed-ended questions. This leaves little room for elaboration and keeps the witness focused on answering directly.

3. **Slow Down to Emphasize Critical Points**:
   - When approaching crucial questions, slow your pace, and maintain eye contact. This signals the importance of the question to both the witness and the jurors, encouraging careful, considered responses.

4. **Use Pauses Strategically**:
   - After important questions, pause briefly. This places pressure on the witness to respond thoughtfully, while also giving jurors a moment to absorb the significance of the question.

5. **Redirect Evasive Responses**:
   - If the witness tries to divert the question, gently bring them back by repeating or rephrasing the question with a controlled pace. For example, "Just to clarify, my question was..." This technique keeps the witness on track without appearing confrontational.

Practical Application: Tempo Control Across Legal Scenarios

1. **Directing a Hostile Witness**:
   - When dealing with hostility, maintain a steady, assertive pace without allowing the witness to gain control through lengthy answers. Increase tempo when needed to keep responses concise.

2. **Emphasizing Critical Testimony in Cross-Examination**:
   - Slow down during questions that reveal inconsistencies or critical points, allowing jurors

to focus on the importance of the response. This also builds suspense, keeping jurors attentive.

3. **Maintaining Juror Engagement**:
   - During complex testimony, use tempo variation to keep jurors engaged. Faster questioning can add energy, while slower pacing at key moments highlights the significance, helping jurors track the case narrative.

Advanced Techniques: Combining Mirroring, Reframing, and Tempo Control for Maximum Effect

Creating a Rhythm That Keeps the Witness Aligned

By combining mirroring, reframing, and tempo control, attorneys can establish a rhythmic exchange that keeps the witness aligned and responsive. For instance, an attorney might begin with mirroring to build rapport, use tempo control to direct the witness's responses, and apply reframing to emphasize points that support the case narrative. This blend of techniques prevents the witness from steering off course, reinforcing the attorney's authority over the examination.

Adapting in Real-Time for Greater Impact

Witnesses often display unexpected behaviors, especially under pressure. Being able to adapt in real-time by switching between techniques—like shifting from a calm tone to a controlled tempo increase or using reframing to turn evasive answers into supportive statements—ensures the attorney maintains authority and control. Mastery of these techniques allows for flexibility, giving attorneys the upper hand regardless of witness behavior.

Practical Scripts: Cross-Examination Techniques in Action

1. **Using Mirroring to Disarm**:
   o Attorney: *[leaning slightly forward, matching witness's tense posture]* "I understand this has been a challenging process. Can you help us clarify the sequence of events from your perspective?"
2. **Reframing to Challenge Evasion**:
   o Witness: "I think that's outside my area of responsibility."
   o Attorney: "So, are you saying you weren't aware of any issues related to this process?" *(Reframes evasive answer to focus on awareness)*
3. **Tempo Control for Emphasis**:
   o Attorney: *[slowing pace]* "Let's go over that once more. You said you saw the document—at what time, exactly?" *(Uses slow tempo to emphasize critical timing)*

Mastering Cross-Examination for Controlled, Impactful Testimony

Effective cross-examination is an art of influence, requiring attorneys to manage both the witness's responses and the jurors' perception of those responses. By using techniques like mirroring to build rapport, reframing to reshape uncooperative answers, and controlling tempo to emphasize key points, attorneys maintain authority and guide testimony in a way that supports their case. Mastery of these strategies ensures that cross-examination is not merely a questioning exercise but a calculated performance that builds credibility, uncovers inconsistencies, and aligns witness statements with the broader narrative of the case.

Subtle Persuasion and Influence Techniques: Guiding Witness Testimony with Precision

In the courtroom, witness responses can significantly shape the narrative and jurors' perceptions. Subtle persuasion techniques, like embedding suggestions and using pacing and leading, allow attorneys to gently guide a witness's responses and influence their demeanor without direct confrontation. By embedding suggestions, attorneys can shape the content of a witness's response, aligning it with their desired narrative. Pacing and leading, on the other hand, subtly control the witness's emotional state, helping shift their behavior or mood to improve testimony clarity and credibility. These advanced techniques provide attorneys with the tools to steer testimony effectively, ensuring that witness statements strengthen the case.

Embedding Suggestions: The Art of Planting Ideas in Questioning

Why Embedded Suggestions Work: Influencing Without Directing

Embedded suggestions allow attorneys to influence witness responses by subtly planting ideas within questions. This technique relies on the psychological principle of suggestion, where the mind responds to implied cues, filling in gaps with the suggested narrative. In cross-examination, where direct influence may trigger defensiveness, embedding suggestions gives attorneys a powerful way to frame responses, encouraging witnesses to provide answers that align more closely with the case's themes.

The Attorney Who Mastered Embedded Suggestions

In a property dispute case, attorney Julia needed a witness to imply that her client had acted responsibly in maintaining the property. Rather than asking directly, which might have led the witness to react defensively, Julia embedded her suggestion into a question: "So, given how my client carefully managed the property, you'd agree that any minor maintenance issues were likely addressed promptly?" By phrasing the question this way, Julia led the witness toward agreement without directly prompting them. The witness's response aligned with her intended narrative, subtly reinforcing her client's diligence.

Step-by-Step Guide: Embedding Suggestions in Witness Questioning

1. **Frame Questions with Assumptive Language**:
   o Use phrases that assume certain facts, like "Since you've seen how carefully the defendant handled this matter..." or "Based on your experience, it seems logical that..."
2. **Use Leading Statements to Set Context**:
   o Start with a statement that frames the situation in a way that suggests a favorable perspective. For instance, "In a well-run organization like yours, it's expected that issues are managed efficiently, correct?"
3. **Incorporate Positive Qualities into the Question**:
   o Embed attributes that reflect positively on your client or negatively on the opposition. For example, "So, when you saw the defendant's considerate approach, it seemed he had everything under control, right?"
4. **Make the Suggestion Seem Like a Given**:
   o Use language that makes the suggestion appear obvious, such as "Naturally, given the situation..." or "It's fair to assume that..."
5. **Repeat Key Phrases Subtly**:
   o Reinforce the suggestion by subtly repeating the key phrase in related questions. For instance, in a negligence case, you might embed "careful and thorough" to imply responsible behavior.

Practical Application: Embedded Suggestions Across Legal Scenarios

1. **Direct Examination to Reinforce Credibility**:
   o Use embedded suggestions to emphasize the witness's reliability, e.g., "Given your extensive experience in this field, would you say this method is the best practice?"
2. **Cross-Examination to Highlight Uncertainty**:
   o When questioning an opposing witness, use suggestions that imply doubt or ambiguity: "So, with all the variables at play, it would be easy to overlook some details, wouldn't it?"
3. **Motion Hearings to Frame Responsibility**:
   o In motion hearings, embedded suggestions can underscore procedural adherence: "As a protocol-focused organization, it's standard to follow up thoroughly, right?"

Pacing and Leading: Shifting Behavior and Mood with Subtle Cues

The Power of Pacing and Leading: Creating Influence Through Rhythm

Pacing and leading involve adjusting your behavior and language to match, then gradually change, the witness's state. "Pacing" mirrors the witness's mood or demeanor, creating rapport and aligning them with your rhythm. "Leading" then subtly shifts this alignment toward a different tone or direction. In witness examination, pacing and leading can help calm a tense witness, energize a passive one, or shift an uncertain witness toward greater clarity. This influence technique enhances control over the witness's responses, making them more responsive to your guidance.

The Attorney Who Shifted a Witness's Mood Using Pacing and Leading

In a high-profile case, attorney Martin was cross-examining a witness who had become visibly anxious, offering hesitant, unclear answers. Martin began by matching the witness's pace, speaking slowly and calmly, mirroring their cautious tone. After a few questions, Martin subtly shifted to a more assertive tone, encouraging the witness to respond with greater confidence. The witness, influenced by Martin's change in rhythm, began answering more clearly and decisively. By the end, the witness was cooperating smoothly, providing the testimony that helped reinforce Martin's case.

Step-by-Step Guide: Using Pacing and Leading to Influence Witness Behavior

1. **Begin by Matching the Witness's Rhythm and Demeanor**:
   - Observe the witness's tone, speed, and energy. Begin questioning with a similar pace, volume, and demeanor to create rapport.
2. **Mirror the Witness's Language Patterns**:
   - If the witness uses certain phrases or terminology, incorporate them into your responses. This reinforces alignment and builds comfort.
3. **Subtly Introduce a Desired Change in Tempo or Tone**:
   - Gradually shift your speech to a faster or slower pace, depending on the goal. For example, if the witness is overly excited, slow down to encourage calm. If they are subdued, introduce a bit more energy.
4. **Use Leading Language to Guide Responses**:
   - Lead the witness with phrases like "As we've discussed..." or "Now that we've clarified..." to

set a steady rhythm that aligns with your desired outcome.

5. **Observe and Adapt to Any Resistance**:
   o If the witness resists the shift, return to pacing briefly before attempting another subtle lead. This process allows the witness to adjust comfortably, maintaining rapport.

Practical Application: Pacing and Leading Across Legal Scenarios

1. **In Cross-Examination with an Aggressive Witness**:
   o Match the witness's intensity briefly, then lead them toward a calmer tone, asking questions that encourage reflection rather than confrontation, e.g., "Let's take a moment to review the events carefully."
2. **Calming Witnesses in Jury Trials**:
   o With a visibly anxious witness, match their slow, hesitant tone initially, then gradually introduce steadier language and reassuring phrases, guiding them to respond with confidence.
3. **Encouraging Detailed Testimony During Motion Hearings**:
   o For witnesses offering brief answers, begin with short, simple questions to match their brevity, then gradually shift to open-ended questions that require fuller answers, subtly encouraging more detailed responses.

Advanced Strategies: Combining Embedded Suggestions, Pacing, and Leading for Maximum Influence

Creating a Cooperative Dynamic with Embedded Pacing

By embedding suggestions while pacing, attorneys can reinforce desired responses without direct confrontation. For instance, with a hesitant witness, mirroring their language while embedding confidence-boosting suggestions, like "You've clearly thought this through…" can shift their responses toward certainty. This layered technique increases influence, blending subtle suggestion with a rhythm that aligns the witness with the case narrative.

Strategic Leading with Repeated Phrases for Emphasis

Combining leading techniques with repeated phrases helps reinforce the influence. For example, an attorney can use pacing to match a reluctant witness, then lead with a repeated phrase like "As we clarified earlier…" to subtly reinforce specific facts. This strategy maintains control while steering the witness toward desired answers.

Practical Scripts: Subtle Persuasion and Influence Techniques in Action

1. **Embedding Suggestions in Direct Examination**:
   o "Based on your experience, it's fair to say this was handled responsibly, wouldn't you agree?" *(Embeds the suggestion of responsibility in the question)*
2. **Pacing and Leading a Nervous Witness**:
   o Attorney: *[initially matching slow pace]* "It's okay, just take your time with this question… Now

that you've had a chance to think it over, could you walk us through your thought process?" *(Uses leading to shift from a hesitant to more confident response)*

3. **Combining Suggestions with Leading Language**:
   - "As you mentioned earlier, you carefully reviewed all the documentation. Given that thorough approach, it would be difficult to overlook any major issues, correct?" *(This combines embedded suggestion with leading to reinforce the narrative)*

Mastering Subtle Persuasion and Influence for Effective Witness Examination

Subtle persuasion techniques like embedded suggestions, pacing, and leading allow attorneys to guide witness testimony in ways that feel natural and unforced. By embedding key ideas within questions, attorneys can frame witness responses to align with the case's narrative. Meanwhile, pacing and leading create a controlled rhythm that enhances witness cooperation and helps direct their emotional state. Mastery of these techniques ensures that witness examination remains both impactful and precisely guided, strengthening the attorney's control over testimony while subtly influencing jurors' perceptions.

As we move into the realm of influencing judges during motion hearings and negotiations, we enter a nuanced area where subtle communication techniques can significantly impact case outcomes. Unlike jury trials, where emotional appeal often plays a larger role, influencing a judge requires precision, professionalism, and an understanding of how to align with and subtly guide their perspective. In this section, we'll delve into methods for establishing rapport through calibrated mirroring and pacing, crafting persuasive arguments with specialized language patterns, and skillfully handling objections and reframes in real-time. Mastering these techniques allows attorneys to communicate with clarity and poise, ensuring their arguments resonate strongly in judicial settings.

8. Influencing Judges During Motion Hearings and Negotiations: Techniques for Effective Advocacy

In motion hearings and negotiations, subtle influence can be invaluable for steering the judge's perception of the case and presenting persuasive arguments that reinforce the intended outcome. This section covers strategies for building rapport with judges, aligning with their style to gain rapport and subtly lead interactions. Additionally, we'll explore language patterns from the Milton Model to enhance persuasive arguments and framing techniques that allow attorneys to present cases with maximum impact. Finally, techniques for handling objections and managing reframes in real-time provide the tools needed to navigate challenges confidently. and effectively.

Establishing Rapport with Judges: Building Connection and Trust in Motion Hearings and Negotiations

Establishing rapport with judges during motion hearings and negotiations is a powerful technique that can enhance credibility and influence. Judges, like any individuals, are more receptive to those they feel connected to, and rapport helps create a collaborative rather than adversarial atmosphere. In the context of motion hearings and negotiations, rapport-building techniques like subtle mirroring and calibration allow attorneys to align with a judge's communication style and non-verbal cues, promoting receptivity to arguments. These skills enable attorneys to foster an environment of respect and trust, ultimately increasing the impact of their case presentations.

Subtle Mirroring: Creating Unconscious Rapport through Posture and Speech

Why Mirroring Matters: The Psychology Behind Rapport-Building

Mirroring is an effective technique rooted in the principle of social psychology, where people feel more comfortable and connected with others who reflect their behaviors, speech, or gestures. When used subtly, mirroring establishes an unconscious sense of alignment, which makes the judge more inclined to view the attorney as cooperative and trustworthy. By matching a judge's posture, tone, and pace, attorneys can foster a sense of harmony, which can create a receptive atmosphere and positively influence the judge's perception of the case.

The Attorney Who Used Mirroring to Build Rapport with a Judge

Consider attorney Rachel, who was handling a complex motion hearing with a judge known for being reserved and formal. Recognizing the judge's demeanor, Rachel adjusted her approach by mirroring his neutral posture and controlled tone. When the judge leaned slightly forward to ask questions, Rachel mirrored the gesture subtly, maintaining eye contact and a composed tone. Over the course of the hearing, the judge appeared more engaged and receptive, nodding as Rachel presented her arguments. By the end, the judge ruled in her favor, and Rachel knew her subtle alignment had helped build the trust necessary to sway the decision.

Step-by-Step Guide: Mirroring Techniques for Building Rapport with Judges

1. **Observe the Judge's Posture and Demeanor**:

- o Begin by noting the judge's posture—whether they are leaning forward, sitting upright, or resting back in their chair. Take note of their facial expressions and hand gestures.

2. **Match the Posture Subtly**:
   - o Adjust your posture to reflect the judge's without mimicking it too closely. For instance, if the judge leans forward, adopt a slight forward lean to signal engagement.

3. **Mirror the Judge's Tone and Pace of Speech**:
   - o Listen to the judge's tone and speed of speaking. If they speak slowly and carefully, match their pace. If their tone is more energetic or assertive, adjust yours accordingly, conveying respect and attentiveness.

4. **Maintain Eye Contact at Key Moments**:
   - o Establish eye contact when making significant points, mirroring the judge's gaze level. This helps maintain the rhythm and flow of rapport, creating a mutual sense of focus and trust.

5. **Use Parallel Gestures Subtly**:
   - o When the judge makes hand movements, incorporate similar gestures, such as a slight nod or open-palm movement. These gestures should be natural and understated, ensuring the rapport remains unforced.

Practical Application: Mirroring Across Different Judicial Scenarios

1. **In Motion Hearings with Reserved Judges**:
   - o For judges who maintain a formal, reserved demeanor, adopt a neutral tone, sit upright, and match their controlled gestures. This establishes an atmosphere of respect and professionalism, conducive to rapport.

2. **Negotiations with Judges Known for Expressive Gestures**:

- o If a judge is expressive with hand movements or body language, incorporate similar gestures, like leaning forward to emphasize a point. This reflects a shared energy and alignment, creating an environment of mutual engagement.
3. **In High-Stakes Arguments with Assertive Judges**:
   - o For assertive judges, mirror their confidence by using direct language and matching their volume or pacing. This shows that you are composed under pressure, earning respect and attention.

Calibration: Adjusting Based on Non-Verbal Cues for Maximum Rapport

Why Calibration is Crucial: Adapting to Dynamic Courtroom Interactions

Calibration is the process of observing and adapting to subtle cues from the judge to fine-tune the interaction. Judges' reactions, especially their non-verbal signals, offer immediate feedback on their engagement level, agreement, or discomfort with the arguments presented. By recognizing and responding to these cues, attorneys can shift their approach, either reinforcing a positive response or softening when resistance is detected. Calibration helps ensure that the interaction remains fluid and adaptive, keeping the judge's attention and encouraging receptivity.

The Attorney Who Calibrated Responses to Adapt to a Judge's Cues

Attorney Michael was in a motion hearing with a judge who initially appeared receptive but began showing signs of impatience as the argument progressed. Michael noticed subtle cues—the judge shifted in his seat, looked away, and crossed his arms. Recognizing the change, Michael adjusted by shortening his responses and focusing on key points, speeding up the tempo slightly to match the judge's impatience. The judge relaxed, uncrossed his arms, and re-engaged with Michael's argument. This calibration allowed Michael to regain the judge's attention and respect, contributing to a favorable outcome.

Step-by-Step Guide: Calibration Techniques for Engaging Judges

1. **Observe Baseline Non-Verbal Cues**:
   o At the start of the hearing, establish a baseline of the judge's non-verbal cues. Are they leaning forward, nodding, or maintaining neutral eye contact? Note any initial signals of interest or disinterest.
2. **Watch for Shifts in Body Language**:
   o As the hearing progresses, watch for changes, such as crossing arms, leaning back, or avoiding eye contact. These shifts often indicate resistance, disagreement, or disengagement.
3. **Adapt Your Responses in Real-Time**:
   o When signs of resistance appear, adjust by simplifying your points or speeding up your delivery. When signs of receptiveness (e.g., nodding, relaxed posture) are present, elaborate slightly, reinforcing your point.
4. **Match Emotional Cues with Tone Adjustments**:
   o If the judge appears empathetic, soften your tone. If they appear analytical, maintain a direct, logical tone. Calibration ensures you are meeting the judge's emotional state, creating alignment.
5. **Reflect Positive Cues to Reinforce Engagement**:
   o When the judge exhibits positive cues like nodding or leaning forward, mirror these cues subtly, adding slight gestures that reinforce agreement. This boosts rapport and encourages the judge to maintain engagement.

Practical Application: Calibration in Various Courtroom Scenarios

1. **Handling Shifts in Judge Engagement During Arguments**:
   o If a judge begins showing signs of disengagement, recalibrate by shortening statements and emphasizing essential points. This respects their time and refocuses attention.
2. **In Negotiations with Multiple Adjustments**:
   o When dealing with complex negotiations that involve frequent changes, adapt to each shift by mirroring the judge's body language and adjusting tone based on cues. This maintains rapport even during challenging discussions.
3. **Managing Judge Disagreement in Motion Hearings**:
   o If a judge shows visible disagreement, use calibration to adjust by pausing, softening your tone, and rephrasing statements in a way that acknowledges their perspective while presenting a new angle.

Advanced Techniques: Integrating Mirroring and Calibration for Stronger Influence

Using Mirroring and Calibration as a Dynamic Influence Cycle

By combining mirroring with calibration, attorneys can establish rapport and then refine it throughout the hearing. Start by mirroring to build initial alignment, then use calibration to adapt responses based on the judge's feedback. This dynamic approach not only builds trust but also maintains the judge's engagement, as the attorney continuously responds to non-verbal cues. For example, begin with mirroring gestures to establish rapport, then calibrate based on the judge's reactions to maintain a steady connection throughout.

Leveraging Calibration to Navigate Challenging Moments

In moments of tension, calibration can be combined with soft mirroring to ease discomfort. For example, if a judge exhibits resistance, calibrate by pausing and adjusting your tone to a neutral or reflective tone. Then, mirror a more composed posture, signaling understanding. This helps de-escalate tension while reinforcing respect, guiding the interaction toward cooperation.

Practical Scripts: Mirroring and Calibration Techniques in Action

1. **Opening Statement to Establish Rapport**:
   o Attorney: *[matching judge's posture]* "Your Honor, as we've seen in similar cases, the court's attention to procedural fairness is key. I appreciate the opportunity to present a brief overview." *(This mirrors tone and posture while subtly reinforcing respect)*
2. **Calibration in Response to Judge's Resistance**:
   o Judge: *[crosses arms, looking away]*
   o Attorney: *[adjusting pace and softening tone]* "I understand this is a nuanced point, Your Honor. Let me clarify briefly to respect your time." *(This calibrates based on the judge's disengagement, showing attentiveness to their cues)*
3. **Mirroring Judge's Tone for Reinforcement**:
   o Judge: *[speaks in a slow, methodical tone]*
   o Attorney: *[matching pace]* "Thank you, Your Honor. It's important that we proceed carefully, just as you noted, to ensure all considerations are addressed." *(Mirrors pace and tone to align with judge's methodical approach)*

Mastering Rapport-Building for Effective Judicial Influence

Building rapport with judges through mirroring and calibration is an essential skill that enhances trust and receptivity during motion hearings and negotiations. By subtly mirroring posture and speech, attorneys create unconscious alignment, fostering an environment conducive to influence. Calibration allows attorneys to adapt in real-time, adjusting based on non-verbal cues to maintain rapport and engagement. Mastering these techniques ensures that interactions with judges are respectful, adaptive, and persuasive, ultimately enhancing the likelihood of favorable rulings and outcomes.

Pacing and Leading Judges: Aligning and Guiding Judicial Interactions

Pacing and leading is an advanced influence technique that begins by aligning with the judge's communication style, tone, and pacing, then gradually guiding the interaction toward a desired outcome. Pacing involves matching the judge's behavior, creating an unconscious rapport by subtly mirroring their style and demeanor. Once this rapport is established, the attorney can "lead" by slowly shifting the tone, pace, or content of the exchange, encouraging the judge to follow. This technique helps attorneys maintain control, particularly in situations where the judge may be initially resistant or undecided, enhancing the receptivity of arguments and requests.

Aligning with the Judge's Style: The Foundation of Pacing

Understanding the Judge's Style: Observing and Adapting to Verbal and Non-Verbal Cues

Aligning with a judge's style begins with careful observation. Judges often have a unique rhythm, tone, and preferred way of interacting in the courtroom, which can range from formal and reserved to more conversational. Understanding these subtleties allows the attorney to mirror this style effectively, creating a natural connection and reducing any perceived opposition. This alignment not only demonstrates respect for the judge's authority but also enhances the likelihood that the judge will be open to the attorney's lead once rapport is established.

The Attorney Who Mastered Pacing to Gain Judicial Support

Consider attorney Mark, who faced a judge known for a direct, fast-paced communication style. During a complex motion hearing, Mark realized that his usual deliberate approach wasn't resonating with the judge. Instead, Mark adjusted by adopting a similar brisk tone and pace, presenting his arguments in concise, punchy statements that matched the judge's style. After establishing this alignment, Mark subtly shifted his language and tone to introduce more nuanced points, guiding the judge's attention to specific details. The judge, now in sync with Mark's rhythm, was more receptive to his arguments, ultimately ruling in his favor. Mark's pacing allowed him to match the judge's tempo, setting the foundation for a successful interaction.

Step-by-Step Guide: Pacing a Judge's Communication Style

1. **Observe the Judge's Rhythm and Tone**:

- o Take note of how the judge speaks. Are they fast and direct, or slow and reflective? Match their tone initially to establish alignment.
2. **Match Speech Patterns and Word Choice**:
   - o Use a similar language style and choice of words. For instance, if the judge uses formal language, mirror this in your responses. If they lean toward informal phrasing, adjust accordingly.
3. **Adopt a Similar Posture and Gesture Style**:
   - o Align your body language subtly with the judge's. If they sit back and speak thoughtfully, mirror this relaxed stance. If they lean forward to engage, do so as well.
4. **Mirror the Judge's Pauses and Timing**:
   - o Pay attention to the judge's use of pauses. If they pause frequently, allow similar pauses in your responses. This rhythm establishes a sense of synchrony, making your arguments feel natural and coherent.
5. **Create a Harmonious Start with Pacing Statements**:
   - o Begin with statements or questions that reinforce alignment, such as, "As you noted earlier, Your Honor…" or "Following the court's earlier perspective on…" This shows attentiveness and demonstrates alignment with their expressed views.

Practical Application: Pacing Techniques in Various Judicial Scenarios

1. **Pacing in Motion Hearings with Reserved Judges**:
   - o For judges who are reserved, match their careful, slower tone, avoiding overly assertive language. This conserves rapport and builds respect, encouraging the judge to remain open to further persuasion.
2. **Aligning in Fast-Paced Negotiations**:
   - o For judges who prefer concise, quick interactions, adopt a brisk pace with succinct

statements. This matching reduces friction and creates a productive rhythm that encourages the judge to engage with your arguments.

3. **Formal Cases with Highly Analytical Judges**:
   - For judges with an analytical focus, mirror their logical approach by presenting arguments in a step-by-step format, aligning with their methodical thinking style and laying the groundwork for gradual influence.

Leading the Judge: Shifting Tone and Direction with Subtle Influence

Why Leading is Effective: Guiding Interaction to Support Argumentation

Once alignment is established through pacing, leading allows attorneys to gradually introduce their own tone, tempo, or viewpoint. This shift can guide the judge's focus toward specific points, making them more open to the case's central argument. By introducing a slight change in tone or perspective, the attorney can guide the interaction, nudging the judge to follow the subtle shift without resistance. Leading must be gradual and natural, preserving the established rapport and encouraging cooperation.

The Attorney Who Led a Judge to Focus on Key Details

In a contentious contract dispute, attorney Anna needed the judge to focus on one particular clause. Initially, she paced the judge's measured, somewhat skeptical tone by emphasizing general fairness and transparency, building rapport. Once alignment was established, Anna began leading by introducing specific language and slowing her pace to emphasize the critical clause, subtly shifting the judge's focus. By the end of her argument, the judge had adopted Anna's tone and pace, centering the ruling on the key contractual detail. This leading allowed Anna to influence the judge's decision without direct pressure.

Step-by-Step Guide: Leading Techniques for Gradual Influence

1. **Introduce Subtle Shifts in Tone**:
   o Once rapport is established, adjust your tone to match the direction you want the interaction to take. If the judge has been neutral, introduce a slight emphasis or energy to highlight key points, leading their attention.
2. **Use Incremental Language Adjustments**:
   o Transition from general terms to more specific, intentional language. For instance, move from "considerations" to "critical factors" when discussing case strengths, subtly framing the argument.
3. **Slow Down During Key Points**:
   o When presenting crucial elements, slow your speech slightly, allowing the judge to absorb the details. This creates a natural lead that encourages the judge to follow and focus.
4. **Introduce Positive Framing**:
   o Lead with phrases that reinforce your argument's validity. For example, "As we both recognize..." or "It's essential to consider..." These frames subtly align the judge's perspective with yours.
5. **Summarize to Reinforce Alignment**:
   o At the end of key sections, use summaries that confirm mutual understanding, such as, "This ensures the case remains consistent with the court's perspective on..." This reinforces alignment while leading the interaction toward a favorable position.

Practical Application: Leading Techniques in Different Judicial Settings

1. **Directing Focus During Motion Hearings**:
   - For hearings with critical points, lead by introducing a deliberate, slower pace as you approach the central argument. This gradual shift prompts the judge to follow and absorb the point's significance.
2. **Guiding Judges in Complex Negotiations**:
   - During negotiations, lead by presenting initial terms with alignment-focused language, then subtly adjust to more specific, assertive phrasing to emphasize critical clauses. This influences the judge's perception of importance without overt pressure.
3. **Shaping Judicial Focus in Technical Arguments**:
   - For technical arguments, begin by aligning with the judge's analytical language, then gradually introduce concrete, critical terms to lead the judge's focus toward specific legal interpretations.

Advanced Strategies: Combining Pacing and Leading for a Seamless Influence Flow

Creating a Harmonious Influence Cycle

By combining pacing and leading, attorneys create an influence cycle where each phase reinforces the other. Start by pacing to match the judge's initial rhythm and communication style, establishing rapport and lowering resistance. Then, gradually lead by introducing slight shifts in tone or language, encouraging the judge to follow naturally. This combined approach ensures the interaction remains smooth, adaptive, and persuasive, increasing the likelihood that the judge will align with the attorney's perspective.

Adjusting Leading Based on Feedback

Leading should always be adaptive, responding to the judge's reactions in real-time. If the judge seems resistant to a shift, return to pacing to rebuild rapport before attempting to lead again. This flexibility allows for an iterative influence process, maintaining rapport while guiding the judge's focus or tone gradually.

Practical Scripts: Pacing and Leading Techniques in Action

1. **Pacing a Judge's Initial Skepticism**:
   - Judge: *[using a formal, measured tone]* "Let's proceed carefully with the details."
   - Attorney: *[matching tone]* "Absolutely, Your Honor. I believe the specifics here are essential. We'll go through each aspect methodically." *(Paces judge's tone, establishing rapport)*
2. **Leading with Focused Language**:
   - Attorney: *[after initial pacing]* "Now that we've reviewed the background, let's consider the core elements impacting this case directly..." *(Introduces a slight emphasis, guiding the judge's focus toward the critical points)*
3. **Guiding Attention During Key Argument Sections**:
   - "As we discuss this, Your Honor, you'll notice how this aligns with existing rulings. It's a crucial element that upholds the standards the court values." *(Transitions from general alignment to leading with critical terms)*

Mastering Pacing and Leading for Judicial Influence

Pacing and leading are invaluable tools for attorneys seeking to guide judicial focus and foster a collaborative interaction during motion hearings and negotiations. By initially aligning with the judge's style through pacing, attorneys build rapport and reduce resistance, creating an environment conducive to subtle influence. Leading then allows attorneys to gradually shift tone or emphasis, encouraging the judge to follow and focus on key arguments. Mastering this technique ensures that judicial interactions remain respectful, adaptive, and ultimately persuasive, strengthening the attorney's influence and improving case outcomes.

Language Patterns for Persuasive Motion Arguments: Crafting Compelling Cases with the Milton Model and Framing Techniques

In legal advocacy, language can be a powerful tool for guiding a judge's perception and subtly influencing their decision-making. During motion hearings and negotiations, persuasive language patterns, such as those found in the Milton Model, provide a framework for crafting arguments that resonate on a deeper level. Additionally, framing techniques shape how cases are presented, emphasizing favorable aspects while downplaying weaknesses. Mastering these advanced language techniques helps attorneys structure their arguments in ways that are compelling, memorable, and persuasive, enhancing the impact of their case presentations in high-stakes judicial settings.

The Milton Model: Structuring Persuasive Arguments with Hypnotic Language Patterns

Understanding the Milton Model: Indirect Influence through Language

The Milton Model, named after the renowned hypnotherapist Milton Erickson, involves using subtle, indirect language patterns to communicate suggestions without overtly directing the listener. This model is often used in persuasive communication because it allows the speaker to guide thought processes gently, bypassing resistance and appealing to deeper reasoning or emotional associations. In a legal setting, these patterns help attorneys structure arguments that allow the judge to reach the desired conclusion independently, reinforcing the perception that their judgment is sound, unbiased, and rational.

The Attorney Who Used the Milton Model to Guide Judicial Perception

Attorney Sarah was representing a client in a complex contract dispute, facing a judge who was initially skeptical about her client's position. Sarah decided to use the Milton Model to structure her motion argument, using language that subtly suggested her client's perspective was the most reasonable outcome. By using phrases like, "As we naturally consider fairness in this context…" and "One would almost expect this level of responsibility under these circumstances…" she gently led the judge's thinking without making direct assertions. The judge, seemingly coming to his own conclusions, ruled in favor of her client, a decision influenced by Sarah's skillful use of hypnotic language patterns.

Step-by-Step Guide: Applying the Milton Model in Motion Arguments

1. **Utilize Ambiguous Language to Allow for Flexible Interpretation**:
   - Start with open-ended phrases that give room for interpretation, like "It stands to reason…" or "In similar situations, we often find…" These allow the judge to form conclusions based on their own reasoning.
2. **Embed Suggestions within Statements**:
   - Use statements that embed suggestions subtly. For example, "As we know, fairness is always the priority…" suggests that your argument is

aligned with the court's value of fairness without directly saying so.

3. **Apply Softening Phrases to Reduce Resistance**:
   - Use phrases that make suggestions feel non-threatening, like "One might consider…" or "It's possible to imagine…" which present arguments as thoughts rather than imperatives.

4. **Use Vague Terms to Allow the Judge to Project Meaning**:
   - Avoid absolute statements, and use words like "perhaps" or "naturally" to give the judge flexibility in their interpretation. For instance, "This approach naturally feels appropriate, given the context…"

5. **Present Conclusions as If They Are Self-Evident**:
   - Instead of asserting conclusions, suggest them as common knowledge. For example, "It's well understood that accountability in these cases supports justice…" This aligns the argument with principles the judge may already value.

Practical Application: Milton Model Techniques in Legal Settings

1. **In Motion Hearings for Judicial Alignment**:
   - Use the Milton Model to subtly align your case with principles the judge values, such as fairness or due diligence, by embedding these values within your arguments.

2. **During Negotiations with Skeptical Judges**:
   - If a judge appears hesitant, use ambiguous language and softening phrases to introduce suggestions that reduce resistance, such as "Perhaps it's worth considering…"

3. **Reinforcing Key Points with Embedded Suggestions**:
   - Reinforce critical case elements by embedding them within statements that appear neutral,

subtly guiding the judge to view these points as reasonable conclusions.

Framing Techniques: Presenting Cases in the Most Compelling Light

The Power of Framing: Shaping Perception through Context

Framing is a technique that involves presenting information in a way that emphasizes certain aspects while downplaying others, shaping the judge's perception of the case. By controlling the "frame" through which information is presented, attorneys can influence how judges interpret facts and arguments. Effective framing helps attorneys position their case narratives as logical, fair, and aligned with judicial values, encouraging favorable outcomes without overtly pushing for them.

Framing a Case to Highlight Integrity and Fairness

In a civil case involving financial negligence, attorney Thomas needed to overcome a biased initial perception. He decided to frame his argument around the theme of integrity, constantly referencing "responsible practices" and "commitment to fairness." By emphasizing his client's commitment to ethical standards, Thomas created a narrative that positioned his client as a model of integrity. The judge, unconsciously influenced by the positive framing, ruled favorably, noting the alignment with "standards of fairness" in her closing remarks. Thomas's framing helped shape the perception of his client's character, ultimately influencing the judge's decision.

Step-by-Step Guide: Applying Framing Techniques in Motion Arguments

1. **Choose a Central Theme that Reflects Favorably on Your Client**:
   - Decide on a primary concept that supports your client's image, such as integrity, fairness, or responsibility. Use this as a foundation to frame the entire argument.
2. **Use Positive Framing to Reinforce Desirable Qualities**:
   - Emphasize qualities that portray your client in a positive light, such as "diligence" or "ethical standards," to reinforce favorable perceptions.
3. **Frame Opposing Arguments in a Way that Highlights Weaknesses**:
   - Use subtle language to frame the opposition's case as less reliable or comprehensive. For instance, "While the opposing view raises interesting points, it lacks the depth of our client's approach..."
4. **Highlight Values Aligned with the Judge's Principles**:
   - Frame your arguments around values the judge prioritizes, such as procedural fairness or accountability. For example, "This approach ensures we're honoring the court's commitment to transparency."
5. **Summarize with Reinforcement of the Framed Perspective**:
   - Conclude by reinforcing the chosen frame, summarizing key points within the context of the positive attributes you've established. For instance, "In light of these responsible practices, it's clear this outcome supports integrity."

Practical Application: Framing Techniques Across Judicial Interactions

1. **Setting the Tone in Motion Hearings**:
   o Begin with a framing statement that sets the stage, such as, "This case is about upholding fairness in procedural matters..." This frames the case around values important to the judge.
2. **Using Framing in Closing Statements**:
   o Summarize with positive framing by reiterating the case's alignment with justice and fairness. For example, "Ultimately, this approach prioritizes accountability and transparency, which are fundamental to this court's values."
3. **Emphasizing Strengths During Objections and Responses**:
   o When responding to objections, frame your response within your chosen theme. For instance, "This objection doesn't undermine our focus on fairness and due diligence..."

Advanced Strategies: Combining the Milton Model and Framing for Maximum Persuasion

Creating a Layered Influence with Embedded Suggestions and Framing

Using the Milton Model within a specific framing context creates a layered approach, where embedded suggestions support the chosen theme. Begin by framing the case with a positive attribute, then reinforce this frame through Milton Model techniques. For example, if the case is framed around "integrity," embed suggestions within arguments that highlight this quality, subtly guiding the judge to view the case in alignment with integrity.

Reinforcing Frames with Repeated Patterns and Themes

Framing is most effective when it is consistent. Reinforce the chosen frame through repeated language patterns and phrases that echo the central theme. For example, if fairness is the frame, consistently use terms like "balanced," "equitable," and "transparent" to solidify the judge's perception. Combined with the Milton Model's embedded suggestions, this approach creates a compelling, consistent narrative.

Practical Scripts: Combining the Milton Model and Framing Techniques

1. **Framing an Argument in Motion Hearings**:
   o "Your Honor, this case fundamentally concerns fairness and transparency. As we explore these elements, it becomes evident that our client's actions were aligned with these values..."
2. **Embedding Suggestions with Framing Language**:
   o "As one considers the diligent steps our client took, it's only natural to view these actions as responsible and aligned with fair practices..."
3. **Summarizing with Framing and Embedded Suggestion**:
   o "Ultimately, Your Honor, the evidence underscores a commitment to integrity that we believe speaks directly to this court's principles of fairness and justice..."

Mastering Language Patterns for Persuasive Judicial Influence

The Milton Model and framing techniques provide attorneys with powerful language tools to shape judicial perception and build persuasive arguments. By using the Milton Model's indirect language patterns, attorneys can embed subtle suggestions that align with their case narrative. Framing techniques further support this influence by positioning arguments within a favorable context, emphasizing values that resonate with the judge. Mastering these language patterns allows attorneys to present cases compellingly and persuasively, reinforcing the case's strengths and guiding the judge's focus in a manner that ultimately supports a favorable ruling.

Handling Objections and Reframes in Real-Time: Navigating Challenges with Confidence and Control

In the dynamic environment of motion hearings and negotiations, attorneys frequently encounter objections or unfavorable rulings that require a quick and composed response. Effective handling of these moments involves real-time reframing and maintaining a controlled, calm state, ensuring that the argument remains persuasive and poised. Techniques for reframing objections turn potential obstacles into opportunities to reinforce the case, while state management helps maintain authority and clarity even under challenging circumstances. Mastery of these skills ensures attorneys can respond confidently, guiding the judge's attention back to favorable aspects of the argument while preserving credibility and control.

Reframing Objections: Turning Obstacles into Opportunities

Understanding the Art of Reframing: Shifting Perspective to Neutralize Objections

Reframing is the technique of taking an objection or unfavorable ruling and presenting it from a new angle that minimizes its negative impact. Instead of treating an objection as a roadblock, effective reframing addresses the judge's concerns while subtly redirecting attention back to the case's strengths. This technique allows attorneys to control the narrative, reinforcing the case's merits while respecting the judge's objections. By rephrasing the objection's context, reframing transforms potentially damaging moments into strategic opportunities to underscore core arguments.

The Attorney Who Reframed an Objection to Strengthen Her Case

During a high-stakes hearing, attorney Jenna faced a judge's objection regarding the relevance of a key piece of evidence. Recognizing that arguing directly might alienate the judge, Jenna chose to reframe the objection, emphasizing how the evidence, though not directly related, provided valuable context that supported the case's overall integrity. She responded, "Your Honor, while I understand the concern over direct relevance, this evidence offers essential context that highlights our commitment to thorough, honest representation." This subtle reframing addressed the judge's objection while reinforcing the narrative of transparency and integrity, ultimately leading to the evidence being considered.

Step-by-Step Guide: Techniques for Reframing Judge Objections

1. **Acknowledge the Objection Respectfully**:
   o Begin by acknowledging the judge's concern to show respect and avoid a confrontational tone. For instance, "I understand Your Honor's concern regarding..."
2. **Identify a Key Value or Theme Relevant to the Case**:
   o Connect the objection to a broader value relevant to your case, such as fairness, integrity, or transparency. Use this value as the basis for your reframe.

3. **Present the Objection in a New Light**:
    o Shift the perspective by reframing the objection as an opportunity to demonstrate the case's strengths. For example, "While it may seem tangential, this evidence reinforces the overall context of due diligence."
4. **Reaffirm the Case's Central Argument**:
    o After reframing, subtly reinforce your case's main theme or argument, bringing the focus back to your desired narrative. Conclude with a statement like, "This context ultimately supports our position on…"
5. **Thank the Judge for the Clarification Opportunity**:
    o Close by showing appreciation, e.g., "Thank you, Your Honor, for allowing me to clarify this point," which further emphasizes respect and composure.

Practical Application: Reframing Techniques in Various Judicial Scenarios

1. **Responding to Relevance Objections**:
    o If a judge raises a relevance objection, reframe by connecting the evidence to a larger narrative, such as "This detail, though seemingly minor, illustrates a pattern of responsible behavior crucial to understanding the case's integrity."
2. **Addressing Concerns over Procedural Fairness**:
    o When facing objections on procedural grounds, frame the objection as reinforcing fairness. For instance, "We appreciate the need for strict adherence to procedure, as it aligns with our commitment to transparency."
3. **Turning Unfavorable Rulings into Reinforcements**:
    o In the case of an adverse ruling, reframe by using the ruling to emphasize the case's strengths. For example, "While the ruling limits this line of evidence, our primary argument

remains strong, focused on the core facts that
are well-supported."

Managing State: Maintaining Composure and Control in Challenging Situations

The Importance of State Management: Staying Calm Under Pressure

State management is the ability to maintain a calm, focused
mental state regardless of external challenges. In the
courtroom, where emotions can run high, this skill is
essential for handling difficult moments, from unexpected
objections to heated negotiations. By managing their state,
attorneys remain authoritative and clear, ensuring that their
arguments are delivered persuasively and that judges
perceive them as professional and credible. Techniques like
controlled breathing, positive visualization, and mental
anchoring enable attorneys to stay grounded, helping them
respond to challenges with confidence and poise.

The Attorney Who Mastered State Management During a Difficult Cross-Examination

Attorney Alex was in the middle of a contentious negotiation
when the opposing counsel raised an unexpected, aggressive
objection. Instead of reacting defensively, Alex took a deep
breath, quickly visualized the successful outcome he had
prepared for, and mentally anchored his calm state. This
allowed him to respond in a steady, composed tone,
addressing the objection confidently. His poise not only
reinforced his argument but also impressed the judge, who
later commented on Alex's professionalism. By maintaining
control of his mental state, Alex navigated a difficult moment
successfully, ultimately securing a favorable outcome.

Step-by-Step Guide: Techniques for Effective State Management

1. **Practice Deep Breathing for Immediate Calm**:
   - When faced with unexpected challenges, take a few slow, deep breaths to reduce physical tension and refocus. Aim for a count of four seconds per inhale and exhale.
2. **Visualize Positive Outcomes Before Entering the Courtroom**:
   - Begin each hearing or negotiation by visualizing a calm, successful outcome. Picture yourself responding confidently to objections, reinforcing a positive mental state.
3. **Use a Physical Anchor to Reinforce Calmness**:
   - Choose a small, discreet gesture (e.g., pressing two fingers together) that you associate with calmness. When facing a challenging moment, use this anchor to recall your composed mental state.
4. **Reframe Negative Thoughts as Opportunities**:
   - If negative thoughts arise, mentally reframe them as opportunities. For example, view an objection as a chance to clarify and strengthen your argument.
5. **Establish a Mental "Pause" for Objectivity**:
   - Before responding, establish a quick mental pause. This can be as simple as thinking, "Pause," to give yourself a moment to assess the situation objectively before speaking.

Practical Application: State Management Techniques in Different Courtroom Scenarios

1. **During Unexpected Objections**:
   - If a judge raises an unforeseen objection, use your physical anchor and take a deep breath. Respond with a steady tone that conveys

authority and thoughtfulness, enhancing your credibility.

2. **Handling High-Stakes Negotiations**:
   - In intense negotiations, maintain composure by visualizing a successful outcome before entering. This preemptive state management creates a mindset of confidence and calm.

3. **Managing Objections from Opposing Counsel**:
   - When opposing counsel raises a pointed objection, view it as an opportunity to reinforce your argument. Use your physical anchor to stay grounded, projecting professionalism.

Advanced Strategies: Integrating Reframing and State Management for Complete Control

Using State Management to Support Effective Reframing

State management and reframing are highly complementary techniques. By maintaining a calm, controlled state, attorneys can approach objections with objectivity and clarity, allowing them to reframe effectively without appearing defensive. For example, if an objection disrupts the flow of your argument, take a brief pause, reframe the objection within your central narrative, and respond confidently. This approach ensures the judge perceives the attorney as composed and solution-oriented, reinforcing their credibility.

Turning Challenging Moments into Persuasive Reinforcements

During heated negotiations or challenging hearings, combine reframing and state management to turn difficult moments into reinforcements of your case. For instance, when a judge expresses frustration over a procedural issue, calmly reframe by acknowledging the importance of procedure while subtly redirecting to your case's commitment to fairness. By staying grounded, you can adapt to the judge's reactions while guiding the narrative back to favorable territory.

Practical Scripts: Reframing and State Management in Action

1. **Reframing an Unexpected Objection on Relevance**:
   - Judge: *[raises objection on relevance]*
   - Attorney: *[takes a breath, maintains calm tone]* "I understand, Your Honor, that this detail may seem tangential. However, it provides context that reinforces the transparency and integrity central to our client's position." *(Reframes to emphasize case strengths)*
2. **Managing State and Reframing in High-Stakes Negotiations**:
   - Opposing Counsel: *[raises aggressive objection]*
   - Attorney: *[uses physical anchor to stay calm]* "Thank you for raising that point. Addressing it allows us to clarify how these considerations align directly with the court's commitment to procedural fairness." *(Uses calm state and reframing to reinforce key values)*
3. **Maintaining Control When Facing Judicial Disagreement**:
   - Judge: *[expresses skepticism]*
   - Attorney: *[pauses, visualizes positive outcome]* "Your Honor, I appreciate the scrutiny. This discussion only strengthens our commitment to ensuring a thorough examination, which is in line with the fairness this court upholds." *(Combines reframing with controlled response)*

Mastering Real-Time Objection Handling for Effective Judicial Influence

Handling objections and reframes in real-time requires a balanced blend of composure, adaptability, and strategic reframing. By reframing objections, attorneys can turn potential setbacks into moments that reinforce their case narrative, maintaining a positive influence on the judge's perception. State management provides the foundation for these techniques, allowing attorneys to respond to challenges calmly and confidently. Mastering these skills ensures attorneys can navigate the dynamic landscape of judicial interactions with authority, creating a favorable environment for their arguments and enhancing the likelihood of positive outcomes.

As we move from courtroom dynamics to the often less formal yet equally critical environment of calendar negotiations, we enter a space where relationship-building and influence take on new forms. Navigating discussions with District Attorneys (DAs) outside the courtroom requires a nuanced approach, where effective rapport-building, persuasive techniques, and reframing skills are essential. In this next section, we'll explore strategies for developing connections with DAs, framing scheduling issues to emphasize mutual benefits, and addressing objections in ways that promote collaboration. By mastering these NLP techniques in calendar negotiations, attorneys can foster productive relationships and secure favorable outcomes while maintaining professional rapport.

9. NLP Techniques for Calendar Negotiations: Building Influence Beyond the Courtroom

Calendar negotiations may seem straightforward, but they offer critical opportunities to build rapport and foster collaboration with District Attorneys. These informal discussions can often shape the trajectory of a case, as flexibility and cooperation on scheduling impact trial preparation and overall case management. In this section, we'll examine advanced NLP techniques designed for calendar negotiations, from non-verbal rapport-building strategies to powerful persuasion methods that highlight mutual benefits. Additionally, we'll cover practical reframing approaches for addressing objections, allowing attorneys to effectively align schedules while fostering positive, ongoing professional relationships with DAs. By mastering these tools, attorneys can ensure smoother, more productive negotiations that support their broader case strategies.

Building Rapport with DAs Outside the Courtroom: The Art of Non-Verbal Influence in Informal Settings

Building a productive and cooperative relationship with District Attorneys (DAs) outside the courtroom can be invaluable for effective calendar negotiations. Establishing rapport in these less formal environments fosters trust and opens the door to smoother collaborations when scheduling conflicts arise. Through subtle non-verbal communication strategies, attorneys can build a positive connection that goes beyond words, influencing the interaction's tone and outcome. Mastering these non-verbal techniques equips attorneys with tools to build rapport naturally, helping create a cooperative atmosphere that benefits both parties.

The Importance of Non-Verbal Rapport-Building Outside the Courtroom

Non-Verbal Cues as Silent Negotiators

In informal settings—whether hallways, phone calls, or brief pre-negotiation meetings—non-verbal communication often takes precedence. In these situations, subtle gestures, eye contact, and posture can convey openness, respect, and cooperation without the need for explicit language. By employing non-verbal cues effectively, attorneys demonstrate their willingness to work collaboratively, often making DAs more open to considering schedule adjustments or other concessions.

An Attorney's Transformation Through Non-Verbal Rapport

Consider Rachel, a defense attorney who struggled with calendar negotiations. She often approached DAs with a firm stance, using direct language and minimal eye contact, which sometimes made interactions feel tense. Realizing the need to change her approach, Rachel began practicing non-verbal rapport techniques, such as open posture and consistent eye contact. At her next calendar negotiation, she nodded in agreement with the DA's initial points and mirrored their relaxed posture, creating an atmosphere of collaboration. The DA responded positively, allowing them to reach a quick agreement on the proposed dates. Rachel's transformation underscored the value of non-verbal rapport, illustrating how these subtle cues can shift the negotiation's dynamic and foster cooperation.

Effective Non-Verbal Communication Strategies for Informal Settings

1. Open Posture: Creating an Inviting and Receptive Presence

Body language speaks volumes in calendar negotiations, and an open posture conveys openness, respect, and interest in the DA's perspective. An open stance—arms relaxed and uncrossed, shoulders back, and torso facing the other person—signals that the attorney is receptive to dialogue, not confrontation. This simple adjustment in posture immediately reduces tension, helping to create a collaborative environment that makes negotiation smoother.

Step-by-Step Guide: Adopting an Open Posture for Rapport-Building

1. **Relax Your Arms and Shoulders**:
   - Keep arms uncrossed and relaxed at your sides or gently resting on a surface to signal openness.
2. **Face the DA Directly**:
   - Position your body to face the DA directly, showing full attention and engagement. This stance shows respect and interest in their perspective.
3. **Lean Forward Slightly When Listening**:
   - A slight forward lean while listening conveys attentiveness and helps foster a connection, encouraging the DA to feel heard.
4. **Avoid Defensive Gestures**:
   - Steer clear of crossing arms, clenching hands, or tapping fingers, which can indicate defensiveness or impatience.

2. Eye Contact: Building Trust and Showing Engagement

Eye contact is a powerful tool for establishing rapport, as it conveys sincerity, confidence, and respect. By maintaining steady, respectful eye contact, attorneys can create a connection that invites cooperation. Eye contact not only builds trust but also encourages the DA to reciprocate attentiveness, making them more receptive to the attorney's points. The balance is key—too much eye contact can be intense, while too little may appear evasive.

Step-by-Step Guide: Using Eye Contact Effectively

1. **Make Initial Eye Contact with a Smile**:
   o Start by making gentle eye contact accompanied by a slight smile, signaling warmth and friendliness.
2. **Maintain Eye Contact During Key Points**:
   o Hold eye contact when discussing significant scheduling needs, as this reinforces the importance of your request.
3. **Use a Relaxed Gaze When Listening**:
   o When the DA speaks, maintain eye contact intermittently, nodding occasionally to show understanding without staring intently.
4. **Break Eye Contact Naturally**:
   o Look away briefly at natural pauses to prevent over-intensity and maintain a relaxed interaction.

3. Mirroring: Subtly Reflecting Non-Verbal Cues to Build Alignment

Mirroring is a technique where one person subtly reflects the other's body language, tone, or gestures. This NLP technique creates unconscious rapport by signaling similarity, making the other person feel at ease. In calendar negotiations, mirroring the DA's relaxed posture, tone, or pacing fosters a sense of alignment, increasing the likelihood of cooperation. Effective mirroring is subtle and should always feel natural to avoid coming across as contrived or insincere.

Step-by-Step Guide: Practicing Mirroring Techniques

1. **Observe the DA's Posture and Gestures**:
   - Take note of the DA's body language. Are they sitting forward, relaxed, or using specific hand gestures?
2. **Match the DA's Tone and Pacing**:
   - If the DA speaks slowly and calmly, match this tempo in your responses. Conversely, if they use a quicker pace, adapt accordingly to stay in sync.
3. **Subtly Reflect Gestures**:
   - If the DA leans back or crosses their legs, mirror this posture without exaggeration. Use similar gestures or nods to signal alignment.
4. **Adapt to Changes in Their Body Language**:
   - If the DA shifts posture or changes their tone, adjust accordingly to maintain alignment and signal receptiveness.

Practical Applications: Non-Verbal Rapport-Building in Different Negotiation Scenarios

Establishing Trust in Initial Interactions

In initial meetings, where impressions set the tone, starting with open posture and eye contact is essential. Greeting the DA with a smile and attentive eye contact shows approachability, making the DA more likely to view the attorney as cooperative and respectful. Establishing non-verbal rapport from the outset creates a foundation for constructive dialogue and cooperation.

Building Alignment in Complex Scheduling Negotiations

When negotiating complex schedules, mirroring becomes invaluable. If a DA expresses frustration about a scheduling conflict, mirroring their tone while maintaining an open, understanding posture can deescalate the situation. For example, if the DA leans back with crossed arms while expressing concern, gently mirroring this posture with a nod of understanding can make them feel heard, creating an opening for a collaborative solution.

Maintaining Rapport in Last-Minute Scheduling Adjustments

For last-minute scheduling adjustments, non-verbal rapport can facilitate understanding. Starting with a slight forward lean, open posture, and sincere eye contact shows empathy, signaling that the attorney respects the DA's constraints. This rapport helps create an environment where the DA feels more comfortable making adjustments or compromises, allowing for productive, efficient resolutions.

Advanced Techniques: Combining Non-Verbal Cues with Verbal Softening Language

Using Non-Verbal Cues to Complement Verbal Phrasing

Combining non-verbal techniques with soft, non-imposing verbal phrasing enhances rapport, especially during delicate negotiations. For instance, using an open posture and gentle eye contact while saying, "I understand if there are constraints on your end; I'd love to explore a solution that works for both of us," reinforces the message of cooperation both verbally and non-verbally. This holistic approach fosters an atmosphere of mutual respect, making it easier to reach agreements.

Creating a Positive Anchor with Consistent Cues

Anchoring is another advanced NLP technique that can be applied through consistent non-verbal cues. If each meeting with a particular DA begins with a friendly nod and relaxed posture, the DA may start associating these cues with productive, agreeable interactions. Over time, these anchored cues become triggers for a cooperative mindset, creating a positive feedback loop that supports ongoing collaboration in future negotiations.

Practical Scripts: Building Non-Verbal Rapport with DAs

1. **Opening a Conversation with Positive Non-Verbal Cues**:
   o Attorney: *[smiling, open posture]* "Good morning! I really appreciate you taking a few minutes to discuss the calendar with me. I know schedules can be tight, so I'd like to explore something flexible."
2. **Mirroring and Verbal Softening in Negotiations**:
   o DA: *[expresses concern about timing constraints]*
   o Attorney: *[mirrors posture, nods]* "Absolutely, I understand that's a consideration. Perhaps we can find an option that aligns with both our schedules?"
3. **Maintaining Rapport in Difficult Adjustments**:
   o Attorney: *[eye contact, slightly leaning forward]* "I realize this is a last-minute request, and I'm grateful for any flexibility. Let's see if there's a way to make it work without putting too much strain on your schedule."

Mastering Non-Verbal Rapport for Productive Calendar Negotiations

Building rapport with DAs outside the courtroom requires a careful balance of non-verbal communication, attentiveness, and respect. Through techniques like open posture, effective eye contact, and subtle mirroring, attorneys can create an environment where collaboration feels natural, encouraging DAs to engage cooperatively. By aligning their body language and tone with the DA's, attorneys foster positive associations that make future interactions smoother and more productive. Mastering these non-verbal strategies ensures that calendar negotiations are more than just logistical discussions; they become opportunities to strengthen professional relationships and promote successful case outcomes.

Persuasion and Influence Techniques for Negotiating Dates: Crafting Collaborative Solutions through NLP

Successful calendar negotiations hinge on the ability to influence and persuade District Attorneys (DAs) while fostering a collaborative atmosphere. Two powerful techniques for achieving this are framing scheduling issues to highlight mutual benefits and anchoring positive emotional states. Framing focuses on presenting scheduling needs in ways that resonate with both parties' interests, emphasizing win-win solutions. Anchoring positive states, combined with strategic language patterns, fosters an environment of cooperation and increases the likelihood of reaching agreeable dates. Together, these techniques make calendar negotiations smoother, more effective, and mutually satisfying.

Framing for Mutual Benefit: Presenting Scheduling Needs with a Collaborative Perspective

The Power of Framing: Turning Scheduling into a Shared Goal

Framing is the art of presenting information in a way that emphasizes shared goals and positive outcomes. When discussing scheduling adjustments, framing focuses on aligning the attorney's needs with the DA's priorities, portraying the proposed dates as beneficial to both parties. Rather than positioning the request as a demand, framing transforms the negotiation into a collaborative discussion. This approach not only reduces resistance but also helps DAs see the value in accommodating the attorney's preferred dates.

Framing for Cooperation in Calendar Negotiations

Imagine attorney Sam, who needed to reschedule a hearing due to conflicting commitments. Rather than simply requesting a change, Sam framed his need in terms of mutual convenience. He said, "By adjusting this date, we'll have additional time to address preliminary issues, which I think will streamline the hearing process for both of us." The DA, who initially seemed hesitant, recognized the value of a more organized hearing and agreed to the change. This story illustrates how framing shifts the focus from individual needs to shared benefits, fostering cooperation.

Step-by-Step Guide: Framing Techniques for Calendar Negotiations

1. **Identify Shared Benefits Beforehand**:
   o Before approaching the DA, think about how your scheduling preference could benefit them.

Examples could include reduced workload on overlapping cases or a more efficient preparation process.

2. **Use Inclusive Language to Emphasize Collaboration**:
   - Replace "I need" with "we can benefit" or "this adjustment helps us..." Inclusive language signals that the negotiation is a cooperative effort, not a one-sided request.

3. **Highlight Specific Advantages for the DA**:
   - Connect your proposed date to benefits for the DA, such as smoother case management or improved efficiency. For example, "This timing allows us both to avoid last-minute conflicts with overlapping cases."

4. **Present Alternatives to Show Flexibility**:
   - Offer a couple of alternatives that still work within your preferred range, showing flexibility. This approach further conveys a willingness to collaborate.

5. **Conclude by Reinforcing the Collaborative Nature of the Solution**:
   - Wrap up by reiterating the mutual benefits of the proposed dates, solidifying the perception of teamwork. For example, "With this schedule, we'll both be set up for a smooth hearing."

Practical Applications: Framing Techniques in Different Calendar Scenarios

1. **When Rescheduling a Hearing**:
   - Start by framing the reschedule as beneficial for both parties. For example, "Adjusting this date gives us both time to resolve preliminary matters, making the hearing more efficient."

2. **For Avoiding Scheduling Conflicts**:
   - Frame the adjustment to prevent conflicts as a strategic advantage, such as "By choosing this

date, we can both avoid case overlap, ensuring a focused hearing."

3. **To Gain Extra Preparation Time**:
   o Present extra preparation time as beneficial to both parties. "With this date, we'll each have the time needed for thorough preparation, leading to a smoother process."

Anchoring Positive States: Creating an Atmosphere of Agreement and Cooperation

Anchoring in Negotiations: Establishing Positive Emotional Associations

Anchoring involves creating a connection between a specific stimulus—such as a gesture, word, or tone—and a positive emotional state. In calendar negotiations, anchoring techniques help foster a cooperative mindset in both the attorney and the DA. By associating specific words or phrases with feelings of collaboration, attorneys can make their requests feel agreeable and mutually beneficial. Anchoring can be achieved through positive language patterns and repeated cues, making the DA more receptive to proposed dates.

Anchoring Positivity to Secure an Agreement

Attorney Lisa was negotiating a series of hearing dates with a DA known for preferring strict scheduling. She used anchoring techniques, repeatedly associating the phrase "smooth process" with collaborative gestures, like nodding and a calm tone. Each time she referenced her proposed dates, she would use the phrase "smooth process" while maintaining steady eye contact and a welcoming smile. Over time, the DA began to respond positively to her suggestions, subconsciously associating Lisa's requests with a smooth, agreeable process. By the end of their negotiation, they had secured mutually acceptable dates with minimal friction.

Step-by-Step Guide: Anchoring Positive States in Calendar Negotiations

1. **Choose a Positive Phrase to Anchor Cooperation**:
   - Select a phrase like "smooth process," "flexible solution," or "best outcome" that reinforces cooperation. Use this phrase consistently during negotiations.
2. **Combine the Phrase with Positive Non-Verbal Cues**:
   - Pair the phrase with friendly gestures, such as a nod, smile, or calm tone. This combination strengthens the association between the phrase and the feeling of collaboration.
3. **Repeat the Phrase at Key Moments**:
   - Use the phrase when discussing your preferred dates, reinforcing the positive association at critical points in the negotiation.
4. **Create Additional Anchors with Reassuring Language Patterns**:
   - Include reassuring phrases like "works well for both of us" or "this option aligns with both our needs" to further anchor the idea of mutual benefit.
5. **Use a Consistent Tone to Reinforce the Anchor**:
   - Maintain a calm, steady tone throughout the discussion to reinforce the cooperative atmosphere and strengthen the anchoring effect.

Practical Applications: Anchoring Techniques Across Negotiation Scenarios

1. **Using Anchoring to Secure Specific Dates**:
   - Pair a phrase like "smooth schedule" with nods and eye contact when discussing your preferred dates. This subconsciously associates those dates with a positive, agreeable outcome.
2. **Anchoring Flexibility in Alternative Dates**:

- When offering alternative dates, use a phrase like "flexible approach" and pair it with a relaxed posture. This reinforces the idea of collaboration even when compromises are made.
3. **Reinforcing Positive Anchors During Objections**:
   - If the DA raises objections, respond with your anchored phrase and calm tone, like "I understand; finding a smooth process here is key," reinforcing the anchor even in challenging moments.

Advanced Strategies: Integrating Framing and Anchoring for Effective Influence

Using Framing to Set Up Anchored Phrases

Combining framing and anchoring techniques creates a layered approach to influence. Start by framing the negotiation around mutual benefits, then use anchored phrases to reinforce those benefits. For example, frame the negotiation by saying, "Aligning on these dates gives us both a flexible solution," then reinforce the idea of flexibility with the phrase "smooth process" at key points. This approach makes the positive frame feel more tangible and reinforces the DA's perception of cooperation.

Reinforcing Anchored States with Repeated Phrasing and Gestures

Consistency is crucial for anchoring. Repeated use of a positive phrase, paired with friendly gestures, creates a strong emotional association. Over time, the DA will begin to associate these verbal and non-verbal cues with agreeable, cooperative outcomes. This consistent reinforcement makes them more likely to respond positively in future negotiations, as they'll subconsciously associate your cues with past successful interactions.

Practical Scripts: Combining Framing and Anchoring for Persuasive Calendar Negotiations

1. **Framing and Anchoring in Date Proposals**:
   o "I think choosing this date will really allow us both a smooth process." *[Nods and makes eye contact]* "This way, we're both set up for success."
2. **Anchoring Flexibility in Alternative Options**:
   o "If that date doesn't work, we have a flexible solution with these alternatives." *[Uses open posture, warm tone]* "It helps us both stay adaptable."
3. **Reframing Objections with Anchored Positivity**:
   o "I understand; finding the best schedule can be challenging. But I think this approach will give us a smooth outcome." *[Maintains steady eye contact and relaxed tone]*

Mastering Persuasion and Influence in Calendar Negotiations

Using NLP techniques like framing and anchoring in calendar negotiations allows attorneys to present their scheduling needs persuasively, emphasizing mutual benefits and reinforcing cooperation. Framing scheduling issues as collaborative solutions ensures that the DA views the proposal positively, while anchoring positive emotional states strengthens receptivity. These techniques not only make calendar negotiations more efficient but also foster ongoing professional rapport, setting the stage for smoother interactions in the future. With practice, attorneys can turn scheduling discussions into constructive, productive negotiations that support both sides.

Reframing Objections and Resistance: Navigating Challenges and Creating Agreement

In calendar negotiations, attorneys often face objections or resistance from District Attorneys (DAs) who are under time constraints or have conflicting priorities. Mastering the skill of reframing objections is key to redirecting these challenges in a way that supports collaboration. By addressing concerns in a positive light and focusing on shared goals, reframing can transform initial resistance into opportunities for mutual benefit. Additionally, techniques like pacing and leading offer a way to gradually align perspectives, helping both parties reach a consensus. These NLP strategies build trust and establish common ground, making it easier to find scheduling solutions that work for everyone involved.

Reframing Objections: Turning Resistance into Collaboration

Understanding Reframing: Shifting Perspectives to Neutralize Objections

Reframing is the process of changing the context or perspective surrounding an objection to reveal a positive or cooperative angle. In the context of calendar negotiations, reframing objections to scheduling changes emphasizes shared benefits rather than focusing on conflict. When DAs resist a proposed date, reframing techniques can highlight how the adjustment supports efficiency, thoroughness, or other mutual goals. This approach makes objections feel less like roadblocks and more like openings for constructive dialogue.

Transforming Resistance with Reframing

Consider attorney Alex, who frequently faced scheduling objections from a DA with a packed calendar. Instead of pushing back, Alex reframed the objection by emphasizing shared benefits. When the DA objected to a proposed date change, Alex responded, "I completely understand your schedule is tight. I think with this adjustment, we'll both have the time to address preliminary issues, making the hearing more efficient for everyone." By shifting the focus to mutual advantages, Alex helped the DA view the change positively, ultimately securing the rescheduled date with minimal friction.

Step-by-Step Guide: Reframing Objections in Calendar Negotiations

1. **Acknowledge the Objection with Empathy**:
   - Start by acknowledging the DA's concern. For example, "I understand this adjustment might seem inconvenient given your current schedule."
2. **Identify a Shared Goal Relevant to the Objection**:
   - Think about mutual goals, like thorough preparation, smooth hearings, or reduced workload. Use these goals as a foundation for your reframe.
3. **Present the Objection as an Opportunity for Improvement**:
   - Reframe the objection in a way that benefits both parties. For example, "Adjusting the date could actually help us both by giving more time to prepare and streamline the case."
4. **Reinforce the Collaborative Nature of the Solution**:
   - Highlight how the proposed solution aligns with shared objectives. For instance, "By working together on this, we're setting ourselves up for a productive hearing."
5. **Express Appreciation for the DA's Flexibility**:

      o Conclude with gratitude, such as, "I appreciate your openness to considering this—it helps us both stay organized."

Practical Applications: Reframing Techniques in Different Calendar Scenarios

1. **When Addressing Last-Minute Objections**:
    o   If a DA objects to a last-minute reschedule, frame the change as beneficial for both sides: "I understand it's short notice, but with this shift, we'll have the preparation time needed for an effective hearing."
2. **Reframing Overlapping Schedules**:
    o   When there are schedule conflicts, acknowledge the concern and frame the adjustment as a way to prevent chaos: "I see this overlap could complicate things. By choosing this date, we can both focus on our respective cases without the added stress."
3. **Turning Preparation Time into a Shared Goal**:
    o   When the DA expresses resistance over a date change due to workload, frame the reschedule as a mutual efficiency move: "This adjustment gives us both the time we need to manage our cases efficiently, ensuring everything is in order."

Using Pacing and Leading: Building Agreement through Gradual Alignment

The Pacing and Leading Technique: Guiding Toward a Shared Solution

Pacing and leading is an NLP strategy that aligns with the other person's current state or perspective before subtly guiding them to a new viewpoint. In calendar negotiations, pacing involves initially acknowledging the DA's stance or concerns, allowing them to feel heard. Once rapport is established, leading gradually introduces new perspectives or solutions, encouraging the DA to consider your proposal without feeling pressured. This technique is particularly useful for managing resistance, as it respects the DA's position while providing a gentle nudge toward agreement.

Leading to Agreement with Pacing Techniques

Attorney Jenna frequently encountered DAs who resisted changing dates. Instead of immediately pushing for her preferred schedule, Jenna used pacing to validate the DA's concerns. She'd say, "I can see why this date seems ideal given your current cases." After establishing rapport, Jenna would introduce her own suggestion by saying, "What if we look at a slightly different timeframe? It could help us both manage the overlap more effectively." This approach made the DA more receptive, often leading to collaborative solutions that worked for both sides.

Step-by-Step Guide: Pacing and Leading Techniques in Calendar Negotiations

1. **Start by Pacing the DA's Concerns**:
   o Begin by reflecting the DA's perspective. For example, "I understand why sticking to this date might seem best given your workload."
2. **Acknowledge the DA's Priorities Explicitly**:
   o Mention specific factors that you know are important to the DA, like efficiency or reduced workload, reinforcing your understanding.
3. **Introduce a Small, Related Change**:
   o After pacing, gently introduce a related suggestion. For example, "Perhaps we could look at shifting just slightly to a date that reduces conflict with other cases."
4. **Gradually Guide Toward Your Preferred Date**:
   o Transition to your preferred date by highlighting its alignment with the DA's priorities: "This date

aligns with our goal of minimizing case overlap and gives us both flexibility."

5. **Conclude with Reinforced Collaboration**:
   o End by reaffirming the mutual benefits: "Working together on this helps ensure we're both set up for a successful hearing."

Practical Applications: Pacing and Leading Techniques for Calendar Adjustments

1. **Pacing Objections to Late Reschedules**:
   o Begin by recognizing the DA's position: "I completely understand the challenge of last-minute adjustments." Then lead by proposing an incremental date shift: "If we look just a few days later, it could help avoid last-minute pressure."
2. **Finding Common Ground with Heavy Schedules**:
   o Acknowledge the DA's scheduling concerns and workload before leading: "I know your calendar is full. How about we explore a day that eases our combined case load?"
3. **Addressing Resistance to Major Date Changes**:
   o Pace by stating, "It makes sense that a larger shift feels difficult right now." Lead gradually by suggesting a minor adjustment that opens the door to your preferred date.

Advanced Strategies: Combining Reframing with Pacing and Leading for Maximum Influence

Using Reframing to Set Up Effective Pacing

Begin by reframing the objection to make it feel less rigid, then use pacing to validate the DA's perspective. For example, if the DA resists a reschedule, reframe by saying, "This adjustment could streamline our schedules." Then pace by agreeing with their scheduling pressures: "I understand there's a lot going on." This combination of reframing and pacing allows the DA to feel heard while opening them to consider new possibilities.

Leading Incrementally for Long-Term Collaboration

In some cases, building rapport through pacing and leading can establish a foundation for future negotiations. Each time you pace their position and lead them to a mutually beneficial solution, you reinforce a collaborative relationship. Over time, the DA becomes more open to your scheduling suggestions as they begin to view you as a flexible, understanding colleague. This creates a positive cycle of cooperation, making future negotiations even more effective.

Practical Scripts: Reframing and Pacing/Leading in Calendar Negotiations

1. **Reframing a Last-Minute Objection with Pacing**:
   - DA: *[objects to a last-minute reschedule]*
   - Attorney: "I understand completely—it's a tight deadline. This adjustment could give us both the chance to avoid a rush." *[paces by acknowledging concern and reframes by highlighting mutual benefits]*
2. **Pacing and Leading to Address Heavy Schedules**:
   - DA: *[expresses frustration with full calendar]*
   - Attorney: "Absolutely, your workload is demanding, and this date change does add pressure." *[paces by acknowledging concern]* "But if we shift slightly, it might actually give us both a bit more breathing room." *[leads by introducing a manageable adjustment]*
3. **Reframing for Shared Efficiency**:
   - DA: *[resists changing the hearing date]*
   - Attorney: "I can see how sticking to that date simplifies things for now." *[paces by validating DA's preference]* "However, by moving it forward, we both have time to organize, which could help

us avoid last-minute issues." *[leads with benefits]*

Mastering Reframing and Pacing for Successful Calendar Negotiations

Reframing objections and employing pacing and leading techniques equip attorneys with advanced tools to handle resistance effectively in calendar negotiations. By reframing objections, attorneys shift perspectives and present scheduling changes as mutually beneficial, creating a collaborative atmosphere. Pacing and leading, meanwhile, establish rapport by aligning with the DA's concerns before gradually introducing alternative solutions. Together, these techniques foster productive, respectful negotiations that help secure favorable scheduling outcomes, supporting efficient case management and professional rapport in the long run.

As we transition into the realm of state management and preparation, we turn to techniques that empower trial lawyers to maintain control over their mental and emotional states while optimizing preparation for trial. This section will cover essential state management strategies to ensure attorneys remain composed and focused, especially under pressure, through visualization exercises and personal anchoring. Additionally, we'll explore NLP techniques for preparing witnesses, allowing lawyers to build confidence and establish positive states in those who testify. Finally, jury selection strategies rooted in NLP will be introduced, offering tools to read and respond to juror cues effectively, ensuring a strategic and adaptive approach throughout the trial process.

10. Mastering State Management and Preparation Techniques for Trial Success

In the high-stakes environment of a courtroom, a trial lawyer's mental and emotional control can make all the difference. Effective state management before and during trials is crucial, enabling lawyers to maintain confidence, focus, and composure under pressure. This section delves into advanced techniques that equip attorneys with powerful tools for self-regulation, such as visualization exercises and personal anchors to bolster mental resilience. Additionally, we'll explore NLP-based methods for preparing witnesses, creating a sense of readiness and calm in those who testify. Finally, we'll uncover strategies for jury selection, utilizing NLP to read juror responses and adapt trial tactics in real time. Together, these skills form a comprehensive approach to trial preparation, ensuring lawyers are mentally equipped, prepared, and adaptive for each stage of the courtroom process.

State Control Techniques Before and During Trials: Cultivating Confidence, Focus, and Composure

Maintaining control over one's mental and emotional state is paramount for trial lawyers. Courtroom dynamics are demanding, and the ability to remain confident, focused, and composed under pressure not only enhances performance but also impacts how others perceive the attorney. Two primary NLP techniques for state control—visualization exercises and personal anchoring—empower attorneys to create these optimal states on demand. Visualization strengthens confidence and clarity, while personal anchors provide quick access to calm and composure during moments of high tension. Together, these methods form a robust foundation for effective state management throughout the trial process.

Visualization Exercises: Harnessing the Power of Mental Imagery

The Science of Visualization: Programming the Mind for Success

Visualization is a powerful mental tool that involves creating vivid mental images of desired outcomes. By repeatedly visualizing specific scenarios, such as delivering a compelling opening statement or handling a difficult cross-examination, attorneys can "rehearse" success, building both confidence and mental preparedness. Visualization engages the brain as if the event were actually happening, strengthening neural pathways associated with positive outcomes and helping eliminate self-doubt. Over time, visualization transforms an attorney's mindset, fostering self-assurance and focus when entering the courtroom.

How Visualization Helped an Attorney Conquer Courtroom Anxiety

Consider Jessica, a young attorney who struggled with anxiety before trials. She decided to try visualization as a means to build confidence. Each evening, she'd close her eyes and vividly imagine herself walking confidently into the courtroom, interacting positively with the judge and jury, and presenting her arguments with clarity and composure. Over time, Jessica noticed a shift; as her mental "rehearsal" of success grew stronger, her anxiety lessened. Visualization became her secret weapon, allowing her to approach each trial with renewed confidence and purpose.

Step-by-Step Guide: Effective Visualization Techniques for Trial Lawyers

1. **Choose a Quiet, Comfortable Space for Visualization**:
   - Sit in a relaxed, upright position. Close your eyes, take deep breaths, and focus on the sensation of calm.
2. **Define Your Goal Clearly**:
   - Identify a specific scenario to visualize, such as your opening statement, cross-examination, or a difficult negotiation. Be as specific as possible, visualizing each detail.
3. **Engage All Your Senses**:
   - Picture the setting, sounds, and sensations involved. Imagine the feel of the courtroom floor beneath your feet, the sound of your voice, and the expressions of the jury or judge as they listen.
4. **Visualize Positive Reactions and Emotions**:
   - Imagine receiving affirming responses, such as jurors nodding in agreement or a witness providing clear answers. Focus on your confidence, calmness, and assertiveness.
5. **Repeat Regularly to Strengthen the Visualization**:
   - Make visualization a daily routine, ideally in the morning or evening. Repetition helps reinforce the mental pathway, making the visualized success more likely to manifest during actual trials.
6. **Use Visualization Immediately Before Entering Court**:
   - Just before entering the courtroom, take a moment to close your eyes and picture a confident, successful performance. This final rehearsal solidifies your focus and boosts your mental state.

Practical Applications: Visualization Exercises for Different Legal Scenarios

1. **For Opening Statements**:
   - Visualize delivering your opening statement with clarity, engaging the jury with your words and expressions. Picture each main point landing effectively, and feel the audience's focus on you.
2. **For Cross-Examinations**:
   - Picture yourself asking questions with confidence, maintaining a calm tone, and watching the witness respond openly. Visualize handling any surprises with ease, maintaining full control.
3. **For Calendar Negotiations and Motion Hearings**:
   - Visualize entering discussions with a DA or judge, presenting your case confidently and respectfully. Imagine a productive, positive outcome and your ability to stay composed and persuasive.

Developing and Using Personal Anchors: Accessing Composure in High-Pressure Moments

The Anchoring Technique: Creating Triggers for Positive Emotional States

Anchoring involves associating a specific gesture, word, or action with a desired emotional state—such as calmness or confidence—so that the state can be recalled instantly in stressful situations. Anchors are powerful NLP tools because they leverage the mind's natural ability to link states with stimuli. For trial lawyers, developing personal anchors creates a mental "switch" that can instantly evoke confidence or composure before a crucial moment, such as a cross-examination or objection.

Using Anchors to Stay Composed Under Pressure

Attorney Michael, who often felt tense during cross-examinations, decided to try anchoring to help him stay calm. During his daily visualization, he added a small, discreet anchor: pressing his thumb and forefinger together whenever he felt the heightened confidence of his mental rehearsal. Soon, this simple gesture became Michael's secret weapon. During a particularly intense cross-examination, he discreetly pressed his thumb and forefinger together, and the calm confidence he associated with the gesture washed over him, allowing him to remain composed and effective throughout.

Step-by-Step Guide: Creating and Using Personal Anchors

1. **Choose a Specific Gesture for Your Anchor**:
   - Pick a gesture or touch that can be done discreetly, such as pressing your thumb and forefinger together or lightly touching your wrist. This will become the trigger for your desired state.
2. **Identify the Desired Emotional State**:
   - Choose the feeling you want to anchor, such as calm, confidence, or focus. Be specific to ensure that your anchor reliably triggers this state.
3. **Evoke the Desired State through Visualization or Memory**:
   - Recall a vivid memory of feeling confident or calm, or use visualization to imagine yourself in an empowering moment. Engage all your senses to make the feeling as real as possible.
4. **Activate the Anchor While Fully Experiencing the State**:
   - While feeling the height of confidence or calm, perform the chosen gesture (e.g., press thumb and forefinger together). Repeat this step several

times, strengthening the connection between the gesture and the emotional state.

5. **Reinforce the Anchor with Repetition**:
   - Repeat this process daily to solidify the anchor. Over time, the gesture will automatically trigger the associated state.

6. **Use the Anchor Before and During High-Stress Moments**:
   - Just before entering court or during a tense moment, activate the anchor by performing the gesture. The linked emotional state will return, allowing you to approach the situation with confidence and composure.

Practical Applications: Using Anchors in Different Legal Contexts

1. **During Cross-Examinations**:
   - Use the anchor immediately before cross-examining a difficult witness to recall a state of calm focus, ensuring you maintain control and clarity.

2. **Before Making Objections or Key Statements**:
   - Activate the anchor before making crucial objections or addressing the court. This technique allows you to convey authority and confidence in your tone and body language.

3. **When Negotiating or Arguing Motions**:
   - Use the anchor during heated discussions with a DA or judge to remain calm and composed, fostering a constructive, persuasive demeanor.

Advanced Strategies: Integrating Visualization and Anchoring for Optimal State Control

Creating Anchors During Visualization for Maximum Impact

Combining visualization with anchoring enhances both techniques. For instance, while visualizing a confident, successful trial scenario, activate your anchor (e.g., pressing thumb and forefinger together). This creates a powerful connection between the visualized state and the physical anchor, making it easier to access that state when needed. By pairing visualization with anchoring, attorneys reinforce their confidence and composure, making these states second nature during actual trial situations.

Anchoring Positive Emotions After Small Successes for Added Reinforcement

Another advanced technique is to reinforce anchors immediately after experiencing small victories, such as a successful objection or a productive negotiation. In these moments, perform your anchoring gesture to further solidify the association between the gesture and positive outcomes. This method strengthens the anchor with real-world success, building a robust foundation for confidence and focus.

Practical Scripts: Combining Visualization and Anchoring for State Management

1. **Visualization with Anchoring Before Trial**:
   o *"As I picture walking confidently into the courtroom, I press my thumb and forefinger together. I can see myself presenting with clarity, engaging the jury, and commanding the courtroom. This is who I am in this moment."*
2. **Anchoring Calm Before Cross-Examination**:

- *"Before I begin my cross-examination, I press my thumb and forefinger together, feeling the calm confidence I practiced. I know I'm prepared, focused, and in control."*
3. **Reinforcing Anchor After Small Victories**:
   - *"After making that successful objection, I press my thumb and forefinger together, solidifying this moment of calm success, so I can access it anytime."*

The Power of Visualization and Anchoring for State Management

Visualization and anchoring provide trial lawyers with powerful tools to manage their mental and emotional states, creating resilience, confidence, and composure in even the most challenging situations. Visualization prepares the mind for success, creating a clear image of confident performance. Anchoring complements this by providing a quick, reliable method to access desired states on demand. When combined, these techniques enhance the attorney's ability to approach each stage of the trial with assurance and focus, transforming state management into a key element of trial preparation and courtroom effectiveness.

Preparing Witnesses Using NLP Techniques: Building Confidence and Positive States

Witnesses often feel immense pressure when testifying in court. Their nervousness, hesitation, or anxiety can affect the clarity and credibility of their testimony. By using NLP techniques to establish positive mental states and create personal anchors, attorneys can help witnesses maintain composure, focus, and confidence on the stand. Anchoring positive states for witnesses ensures they can access these emotions even during challenging questions or cross-examination. This section explores step-by-step methods to equip witnesses with these mental tools, empowering them to testify with calm assurance.

Establishing Positive States in Witnesses: The Foundation of Effective Testimony

The Importance of Positive Emotional States for Witness Testimony

Positive emotional states such as confidence, calmness, and focus are vital for witnesses. When a witness feels calm and confident, they are more likely to communicate clearly, remember details accurately, and respond well under pressure. Conversely, states of anxiety or self-doubt can lead to unclear or inconsistent testimony, impacting their credibility in the eyes of the jury. By establishing positive states, attorneys can ensure their witnesses present themselves in the best possible light, enhancing the persuasiveness of their statements.

Building Confidence in a Nervous Witness

Consider an attorney preparing a key witness, Sarah, who felt anxious about her upcoming testimony. Sarah was worried that she would forget important details or get overwhelmed by cross-examination. To address this, the attorney used NLP anchoring techniques, helping Sarah associate feelings of calm and clarity with a simple physical gesture. When she eventually took the stand, she used her anchor to recall her calm state, delivering a clear and composed testimony that resonated well with the jury.

Step-by-Step Guide: Establishing Positive States in Witnesses

1. **Begin by Building Rapport and Creating a Safe Environment**:

o Start by establishing rapport with the witness. Use a calm tone, make eye contact, and engage in light conversation to put them at ease. This initial connection is essential for the witness to feel comfortable and receptive.

2. **Explain the Purpose of Anchoring and Positive States**:
   o Briefly explain the anchoring process and how it will help them feel more confident. Emphasize that this technique is designed to support them during testimony by helping them maintain calm and focus.

3. **Identify a Positive Memory or Experience**:
   o Ask the witness to recall a time when they felt calm, confident, or successful. Guide them to remember details about this experience, asking questions like, "What were you doing?" and "How did you feel?" This helps the witness re-experience the positive state they will later anchor.

4. **Engage All Senses to Strengthen the Positive State**:
   o Encourage the witness to remember sounds, sights, or even smells from that positive memory. For example, "Can you picture where you were? What could you hear?" This multi-sensory recall makes the positive state more vivid, strengthening its impact.

5. **Introduce the Physical Anchor**:
   o Ask the witness to perform a small, discreet action—such as pressing their thumb and forefinger together or gently tapping their wrist. This action will serve as the anchor for the positive state. Instruct the witness to perform this gesture while they fully experience the positive feelings from their memory.

6. **Repeat to Reinforce the Anchor**:
   o Guide the witness through this process several times. Each time, encourage them to evoke the positive memory, fully immerse themselves in the experience, and activate the anchor gesture.

Repetition strengthens the link between the anchor and the positive state.

7. **Test the Anchor to Ensure It's Effective**:
   - After several rounds, ask the witness to perform the anchor gesture without recalling the memory. If the anchor has been established effectively, the witness should feel the positive state return naturally. Reinforce the anchor if necessary by guiding them through additional rounds.

8. **Instruct the Witness to Use the Anchor During Testimony**:
   - Explain that if they feel nervous or unfocused on the stand, they can use the anchor gesture to recall the positive state. This provides a reliable mental tool for remaining calm, confident, and composed throughout their testimony.

Practical Applications: Using Anchors for Different Types of Witnesses

1. **For First-Time Witnesses**:
   - Anchoring calmness is particularly valuable for those unfamiliar with courtroom procedures. Guide them to remember a time they felt at ease in a new situation, and help them link this feeling to their anchor.

2. **For Witnesses Facing Hostile Cross-Examination**:
   - Anchoring confidence is crucial for witnesses likely to face challenging questions. Encourage them to remember a time they handled conflict well, linking this feeling to the anchor to evoke resilience under pressure.

3. **For Expert Witnesses**:
   - Experts may benefit from anchoring focus, particularly when explaining complex information. Help them recall a time when they felt particularly knowledgeable and clear, linking

this state to their anchor for clarity during detailed explanations.

Advanced Strategies: Fine-Tuning the Anchor for Maximum Effectiveness

Creating Multiple Anchors for Different States

In some cases, it may be beneficial to establish multiple anchors for different emotional states. For example, one anchor can be used for calmness, while another can help the witness recall focus. By using multiple anchors, the witness gains flexibility and control over their mental state, choosing the one most suitable for the situation they face on the stand.

Reinforcing Anchors During Trial Preparation

The effectiveness of an anchor improves with reinforcement. During trial preparation, regularly guide the witness through their anchor routines, strengthening the mental association. This ongoing reinforcement helps ensure the anchor remains reliable when the witness needs it most, even in high-stress moments.

Practical Scripts: Anchoring Positive States in Witnesses

1. **Establishing Calm for Testimony**:
   - "Close your eyes and remember a time when you felt completely at ease. Picture yourself there— what can you see? What can you hear? Now, as you feel that calmness, gently press your thumb and forefinger together. Hold onto that calmness while you do this."
2. **Anchoring Confidence for Cross-Examination**:
   - "Think back to a moment when you felt strong and in control. Maybe it was a presentation you

delivered, or a time you stood up for yourself. As you remember that feeling, tap your wrist gently. Let that confidence flow through you each time you tap."

3. **Creating a Focus Anchor for Complex Testimony**:
   - "Imagine a time when you felt focused and clear. Picture what you were doing, and feel that clarity. As you focus, press your thumb and forefinger together. That focus will return whenever you use this anchor."

Addressing Challenges: Ensuring Witnesses are Comfortable with the Anchor

Reassuring Witnesses About the Process

Some witnesses may feel unsure about using mental techniques. Reassure them that anchors are simple tools designed to support them in court and that they'll have full control over how and when to use them. Emphasize that these techniques are private and can be performed subtly, which often helps witnesses feel more comfortable with the process.

Reinforcing the Anchor if Nerves Persist

If a witness still feels nervous despite using their anchor, guide them through additional rounds of reinforcement. Encourage them to practice the anchor daily leading up to the trial, which further strengthens the association and ensures that they'll have access to the calm or focus they need.

Practical Applications: Reinforcing Anchors During Trial Preparation

1. **Practicing Testimony in Mock Scenarios**:

- o Simulate courtroom scenarios, such as cross-examination, and encourage the witness to use their anchor when they start to feel nervous or unsure. This practice familiarizes them with the process of using their anchor under pressure.

2. **Daily Reinforcement Routine**:
   - o Encourage the witness to practice their anchor each morning and evening leading up to the trial. This daily reinforcement builds a strong mental association, making the anchor more effective when needed.

3. **Role-Playing High-Stress Situations**:
   - o If the witness is likely to face challenging questions, role-play scenarios in which they use their anchor to maintain calmness or confidence. This rehearsal solidifies the anchor's effectiveness in real trial situations.

Empowering Witnesses with Anchoring and Positive States

Anchoring positive emotional states in witnesses provides trial lawyers with a powerful tool to support their case. Through this process, witnesses gain access to states of calm, confidence, and focus, empowering them to present their testimony effectively, even under pressure. By following a structured approach, including rapport-building, visualization, and reinforcement, attorneys can help witnesses feel prepared and resilient. Anchoring offers a private and reliable technique that allows witnesses to maintain composure and clarity throughout their testimony, strengthening the impact of their statements and enhancing the attorney's case in the eyes of the jury.

Jury Selection and NLP: Understanding and Influencing Juror Perceptions

Jury selection, or voir dire, is one of the most critical phases in a trial. The ability to read and interpret juror responses, both verbal and non-verbal, allows attorneys to identify potential biases, gauge receptiveness, and select jurors who are likely to view the case favorably. Using NLP techniques, trial lawyers can sharpen their observation skills, paying close attention to subtle cues that reveal a juror's internal responses. By recognizing and interpreting these signals, attorneys can adjust their strategy accordingly to build rapport, clarify biases, and ultimately secure a jury composition that strengthens their position.

Techniques for Reading Juror Responses: Understanding Verbal and Non-Verbal Cues

Recognizing Non-Verbal Cues: Uncovering Hidden Juror Reactions

Jurors communicate as much through their body language as they do through their words. Subtle shifts in posture, eye movements, facial expressions, and breathing patterns often reveal jurors' comfort levels, interest, or potential biases. By becoming adept at reading these cues, attorneys can discern which jurors may be sympathetic, neutral, or biased against their case. This ability to interpret non-verbal signals gives attorneys a significant advantage, allowing them to adapt their questions and adjust their approach.

How Non-Verbal Cues Helped Uncover Bias

Consider attorney Mark, who was representing a defendant in a high-profile case. During jury selection, one potential juror responded neutrally to questions, but Mark noticed subtle signs of discomfort: crossed arms, tightened lips, and downward glances. Sensing unease, he adjusted his questions to probe further, eventually uncovering a bias against his client's background. By observing these non-verbal cues, Mark was able to dismiss this juror, selecting others who appeared more receptive.

Step-by-Step Guide: Reading Non-Verbal Cues During Jury Selection

1. **Observe Baseline Behavior**:
   - Establish each juror's baseline body language by observing them as they wait and listen. This will help you notice when their behavior changes in response to specific questions or topics.
2. **Watch for Signs of Discomfort or Resistance**:
   - Notice any shifts in posture (such as crossing arms or leaning away) and micro-expressions (such as frowning or tightening the jaw). These signals often indicate discomfort, hesitation, or negative judgment.
3. **Identify Signs of Interest and Agreement**:
   - Positive non-verbal cues, like leaning forward, nodding, or uncrossing arms, can suggest openness, engagement, or agreement. Pay attention to these signals, as they indicate jurors who may be more sympathetic.
4. **Note Eye Movements and Blink Rate**:
   - Quick or frequent blinking may indicate nervousness, while steady eye contact usually signals confidence. Eye movement direction (e.g., looking left or right) can also reveal how the juror is processing information, which we'll explore further in reading eye accessing cues.
5. **Interpret Breathing Patterns**:
   - Slowed or deepened breathing suggests relaxation, while shallow, rapid breathing can indicate stress or discomfort.

Practical Applications: Reading Non-Verbal Cues for Jury Selection

1. **When Gauging Receptiveness to Case Details**:
   - If a juror leans forward with open posture when hearing certain details, this suggests interest or agreement. These individuals may be more receptive to your arguments.
2. **Spotting Potential Bias or Prejudice**:
   - Jurors who respond to certain topics with crossed arms or tightened expressions may have underlying biases. Use follow-up questions to probe their beliefs further.
3. **Distinguishing Nervousness from Neutrality**:
   - Rapid blinking or averted eye contact can reveal nervousness about the process, not necessarily bias. Understanding this distinction allows you to focus follow-up questions accordingly.

Adjusting Strategy Based on Non-Verbal Cues: Adapting to Juror Responses

The Adaptive Approach: Using Feedback Loops in Voir Dire

In NLP, adaptive strategies involve responding to observed cues in real-time to create a feedback loop. By observing juror responses and adjusting your approach, you can either reassure or clarify positions, making jurors feel understood and more likely to open up. This adaptability during voir dire fosters rapport and allows attorneys to address concerns proactively, even uncovering information that may not be apparent from verbal responses alone.

Adapting Strategy to Ease a Nervous Juror

Attorney Laura noticed a young juror who seemed hesitant, avoiding eye contact and displaying nervous body language.

Instead of pressing her, Laura softened her tone and explained the role jurors play in upholding justice. The juror visibly relaxed, uncrossing her arms and making eye contact. This shift allowed Laura to ask more direct questions and uncover that the juror, though initially nervous, held no biases and was open to the case.

Step-by-Step Guide: Adapting Strategy Based on Observed Cues

1. **Gauge Receptiveness and Adjust Your Tone**:
   - If a juror appears tense or defensive, use a softer, more inviting tone. Conversely, if a juror seems overly confident or dominant, ask more probing questions to balance the interaction.
2. **Provide Reassurance for Nervous Jurors**:
   - If a juror shows signs of nervousness (e.g., averted gaze, closed posture), acknowledge their role in a positive light and explain that honesty is all you're seeking. This reassurance can relax them and encourage more open responses.
3. **Ask Clarifying Questions for Discrepant Cues**:
   - If a juror's non-verbal cues conflict with their verbal answers, ask follow-up questions to clarify. For example, if they express neutrality but show clear discomfort, gently probe their true feelings.
4. **Use Summarization to Validate Juror Concerns**:
   - After observing discomfort or confusion, summarizing the juror's responses can help validate their feelings. For instance, "It sounds like you have concerns about the time commitment, is that correct?"
5. **Switch Questioning Styles Based on Feedback**:
   - If certain questions seem to resonate positively, ask similar questions to build rapport. If a question causes defensiveness, switch to more open-ended inquiries that invite the juror to share comfortably.

Practical Applications: Adaptive Techniques in Voir Dire

1. **When Addressing Jurors with Conflicting Cues**:
   - If a juror verbally states no bias but shows signs of unease, acknowledge their role and ask questions that give them room to express hidden concerns.
2. **For Jurors Expressing Uncertainty**:
   - For jurors who appear hesitant, shift from direct questioning to hypothetical scenarios, making it easier for them to explore their perspectives without feeling pressured.
3. **Adapting to Diverse Personalities**:
   - Some jurors may respond better to direct questions, while others prefer conversational approaches. Adapt your questioning style to match the individual, showing attentiveness and respect.

Reading Eye Accessing Cues: Decoding Juror Thought Patterns

Eye Accessing Cues: Insight into Juror Processing

Eye accessing cues are a specific NLP technique where eye movements reveal how a person processes information. For example, looking up may indicate visual processing, while looking to the side often signifies auditory processing. In jury selection, these cues provide valuable insights, especially when responses seem rehearsed or unclear. Observing eye patterns helps attorneys understand whether jurors are recalling actual memories, constructing responses, or experiencing emotional reactions, allowing for more targeted questioning.

Using Eye Accessing Cues to Detect Uncertainty

Attorney James noticed that a juror frequently looked to the side while answering questions about past experiences. Recognizing this as an auditory cue (indicating they were likely "hearing" a pre-rehearsed narrative), James followed up with questions that required visual recall. The juror's hesitancy in providing detailed responses revealed uncertainty, allowing James to probe for biases that hadn't been initially apparent.

Step-by-Step Guide: Observing and Interpreting Eye Accessing Cues

1. **Establish a Baseline by Observing Neutral Responses**:
   - Begin by asking neutral questions, such as, "How long have you lived in this city?" Observe the juror's natural eye movements to establish a baseline for comparison.
2. **Watch for Consistent Patterns in Eye Movements**:
   - Note any recurring eye movements, such as looking up or to the side. These patterns often indicate how the juror processes information (visual, auditory, kinesthetic).
3. **Tailor Questions to Different Processing Styles**:
   - If a juror frequently looks up (visual processing), ask questions that encourage visualization, such as "Can you picture a situation where...?" If they look to the side (auditory), focus on hypothetical scenarios.
4. **Probe for Emotional Reactions with Downward Eye Movements**:
   - If a juror's eyes move downward, this often signals emotional or kinesthetic processing. Questions that explore feelings or values may elicit more genuine responses in this state.
5. **Cross-Reference Eye Cues with Body Language and Verbal Responses**:

o   Use eye accessing cues in combination with other non-verbal signals to gain a fuller understanding of juror responses, creating a multi-dimensional picture of their reactions.

Practical Applications: Using Eye Cues in Voir Dire and Jury Management

1. **For Identifying Authentic Responses**:
   o   Eye accessing cues help discern when jurors are recalling genuine experiences versus constructed answers. Use this to target potential biases and clarify responses.
2. **In Complex Emotional Questions**:
   o   When discussing sensitive topics, observe if jurors look downward, indicating kinesthetic or emotional processing. Adjust your questions to respect their emotional state, fostering open dialogue.
3. **During Post-Selection Observation**:
   o   Eye cues are also valuable during trial. Watch for similar patterns in jurors during testimony, as these provide ongoing insights into their receptivity and engagement with the case.

Mastering NLP in Jury Selection for Effective State Management

Using NLP techniques in jury selection enables attorneys to gain a nuanced understanding of juror personalities, biases, and responsiveness. Through reading non-verbal cues, adapting strategy in real-time, and leveraging eye accessing cues, attorneys can build rapport, identify potential biases, and make strategic adjustments to better engage the jury. This approach turns jury selection into a dynamic, responsive process that goes beyond verbal answers, uncovering deeper insights into juror perspectives. By mastering these skills, attorneys enhance their ability to shape jury dynamics, ensuring they enter trial with a jury aligned as closely as possible with their case strategy.

Sources

1. Foundations of NLP

- **Books:**
    - Bandler, R., & Grinder, J. (1979). *Frogs Into Princes: Neuro Linguistic Programming.* Real People Press.
        - Covers the fundamental principles and origins of NLP.
    - O'Connor, J., & Seymour, J. (2002). *Introducing NLP: Psychological Skills for Understanding and Influencing People.* HarperCollins.
        - Discusses the NLP communication model and its relevance across fields.
- **Academic Articles:**
    - Tosey, P., & Mathison, J. (2009). "Neuro-Linguistic Programming: A Critical Appreciation for Managers and Developers." *Management Learning,* 40(4), 437-452.
        - A scholarly perspective on the key principles of NLP.

2. Building Rapport and Influencing Others

- **Books:**
    - Charvet, S. R. (1997). *Words That Change Minds: Mastering the Language of Influence.* Kendall/Hunt Publishing.
        - Explores techniques for mirroring, matching, and building rapport.
    - Andreas, S., & Andreas, C. (1989). *Heart of the Mind: Engaging Your Inner Power to Change with NLP.* Real People Press.
        - Provides insights on pacing and leading techniques and how to build rapport.
- **Articles:**

- Wake, L. (2010). "NLP Principles in Building Rapport with Clients." *The International Journal of NLP & Coaching*, 1(1).
    - Discusses the importance of non-verbal communication and rapport-building strategies.

3. Language Patterns and Persuasion Techniques

- **Books:**
    - Bandler, R., & Grinder, J. (1982). *Reframing: Neuro-Linguistic Programming and the Transformation of Meaning.* Real People Press.
        - Covers reframing techniques, including context and content reframing.
    - Laborde, G. Z. (1987). *Influencing with Integrity: Management Skills for Communication and Negotiation.* Crown House Publishing.
        - Discusses chunking and persuasion techniques relevant to negotiation and communication.
- **Research Papers:**
    - McDermott, I., & O'Connor, J. (2001). *Practical NLP for Managers.* Piatkus Books.
        - A practical guide focusing on language patterns like the Milton and Meta models.

4. Anchoring Emotional States

- **Books:**
    - Dilts, R. (1998). *The Encyclopedia of Systemic NLP and NLP New Coding.* Meta Publications.
        - Detailed discussion on the anchoring process, including creating and collapsing anchors.
    - Grinder, J., & Bostic St. Clair, C. (2001). *Whispering in the Wind.* J & C Enterprises.

- Advanced exploration of anchoring techniques in professional and personal contexts.
- **Articles:**
  - Knight, S. (2009). "Anchoring Techniques in NLP: A Guide for Practitioners." *NLP World Journal,* 14(3).
    - An in-depth guide on anchoring and its applications.

5. Advanced Non-Verbal Techniques

- **Books:**
  - Pease, A., & Pease, B. (2004). *The Definitive Book of Body Language.* Bantam.
    - Discusses non-verbal communication, calibration, and interpreting micro-expressions.
  - Navarro, J. (2008). *What Every Body is Saying: An Ex-FBI Agent's Guide to Speed-Reading People.* Harper Collins.
    - Techniques for reading body language and using pattern interrupts.
- **Articles:**
  - Ekman, P., & Friesen, W. V. (1969). "Nonverbal Leakage and Clues to Deception." *Psychiatry,* 32(1), 88-106.
    - Academic insights into sensory acuity and calibration.

6. Managing Juror Perceptions and Emotions

- **Books:**
  - Ross, D. (2012). *Trial Advocacy: Planning, Analysis, and Strategy.* LexisNexis.
    - Focuses on jury management techniques, including storytelling and non-verbal influence.

- o Zahavy, S. (2016). *Jury Whispering: Using NLP to Persuade Jurors.* Influence Publishing.
  - Specialized NLP techniques for influencing jurors without direct interaction.
- **Articles:**
  - o Finkelstein, B., & Hawthorne, K. (2010). "Jury Dynamics: Managing Juror Perceptions Through NLP Techniques." *Journal of Trial Practice,* 7(2).
    - Detailed analysis of storytelling and perception management.

7. Techniques for Witness Examination

- **Books:**
  - o Lubet, S. (2015). *Modern Trial Advocacy: Analysis and Practice.* National Institute for Trial Advocacy.
    - Includes techniques for building rapport and managing witness states.
  - o Cialdini, R. (2006). *Influence: The Psychology of Persuasion.* Harper Business.
    - Covers persuasion strategies applicable during cross-examination and witness management.
- **Articles:**
  - o Pennington, N., & Hastie, R. (1986). "Evidence Evaluation in Complex Decision Making." *Journal of Personality and Social Psychology,* 51(2), 242-258.
    - Insights into influencing and evaluating witness responses.

8. Influencing Judges During Motion Hearings and Negotiations

- **Books:**
  - o Lubet, S. (2009). *Excellence in Advocacy: Techniques and Strategies for Persuasive Argument.* LexisNexis.

- Techniques for influencing judges using persuasive language patterns.
  - o Jory, R. (2013). *Effective Negotiation: A Guide for Defense Lawyers.* Thomson Reuters.
    - NLP strategies adapted for negotiating with judges and DAs.
- **Articles:**
  - o Bruce, C. (2011). "The Persuasive Lawyer: Using NLP in Legal Arguments." *The Legal Practitioner's Journal,* 23(4).
    - Application of NLP persuasion techniques in legal settings.

9. NLP Techniques for Calendar Negotiations

- **Books:**
  - o Ury, W. L., & Fisher, R. (2011). *Getting to Yes: Negotiating Agreement Without Giving In.* Penguin Books.
    - Techniques on rapport-building and persuasion during negotiations.
  - o Covey, S. R. (1989). *The 7 Habits of Highly Effective People.* Free Press.
    - Focuses on negotiation and communication skills, including finding win-win solutions.
- **Articles:**
  - o Thomas, K. (2008). "The Art of Legal Negotiation: Techniques for Effective Scheduling." *Journal of Law & Practice,* 15(1).
    - Explores techniques specifically for calendar negotiations.

10. State Management and Preparation Techniques for Trial Lawyers

- **Books:**
  - o Robbins, A. (2001). *Awaken the Giant Within: How to Take Immediate Control of Your Mental,*

Emotional, Physical, and Financial Destiny!. Free Press.
  - Techniques for state management, including visualization and anchoring.
- Bandler, R. (1993). *Time for a Change*. Meta Publications.
  - Advanced methods for state control and mental preparation.

- **Articles:**
  - Dilts, R., & McDonald, A. (1997). "NLP Strategies for Confidence in High-Stakes Situations." *Journal of NLP Research*, 9(2).
    - Focuses on mental preparation and confidence-building techniques.

Additional Comprehensive Resources

- **Books:**
  - Andreas, S., & Faulkner, C. (1994). *NLP: The New Technology of Achievement*. HarperOne.
    - A comprehensive guide covering multiple NLP techniques applicable in law.
  - Collins, P. (2008). *The NLP Coach: A Comprehensive Guide to Personal Well-Being & Professional Success*. Piatkus Books.
    - General NLP coaching techniques that can be adapted to trial lawyering.
- **Academic Compilations:**
  - Dilts, R., & DeLozier, J. (2000). *NLP II: The Next Generation*. Meta Publications.
    - An advanced exploration of NLP methodologies for experienced practitioners.

www.ingramcontent.com/pod-product-compliance
Lightning Source LLC
Chambersburg PA
CBHW071734270326
41928CB00013B/2674